La
Paella

La Paella

Recipes for delicious Spanish rice and noodle dishes

Louise Pickford

photography by Ian Wallace

RYLAND PETERS & SMALL
LONDON • NEW YORK

Designer Paul Stradling
Editor Sarah Vaughan
Production Mai-ling Collyer
Art Director Leslie Harrington
Editorial Director Julia Charles
Publisher Cindy Richards

Food and prop stylist Louise Pickford
Indexer Vanessa Bird

First published in 2020
by Ryland Peters & Small,
20–21 Jockey's Fields,
London WC1R 4BW
and
341 E 116th St,
New York NY 10029

www.rylandpeters.com

10 9 8 7 6 5

Notes

• Both British (Metric) and American (Imperial plus US cup) measurements are included in these recipes for your convenience – however it is important to work with one set of measurements and not alternate between the two within a recipe.

• All spoon measurements are level unless specified.

• All eggs are medium (UK) or large (US), unless specified as large, in which case US extra-large should be used. Uncooked or partially cooked eggs should not be served to the elderly or frail, young children, pregnant women or those with compromised immune systems.

• Ovens should be preheated to the specified temperatures. We recommend using an oven thermometer. If using a fan-assisted oven, adjust temperatures according to the manufacturer's instructions.

• When a recipe calls for the grated zest of citrus fruit, buy unwaxed fruit and wash well before using. If you can only find treated fruit, scrub well in warm soapy water before using.

Contents

Introduction

This book celebrates one of the most loved and perhaps well known Spanish dishes, paella. While most of us know rice to be the basis of this delicious dish, a lesser known type of pasta noodle, called fideo (or fideu in Catalan), is also cooked in a similar way. The dish is known as fideua (pronounced fi-de-gwah) and means 'a large amount of noodles'.

Deeply rooted in Spanish culture and cuisine, rice was first introduced by the Arabs in the 8th century. Now, it is one of the country's most important food sources. Today, Spain is Europe's second largest rice producer; the low-lying wetland areas of Valencia, Murcia and Catalonia boasting perfect conditions for paella rice to thrive. Highly regarded for its ability to absorb up to three times its volume in liquid, the rice swells as it cooks while retaining its shape and texture. It is harder to decipher when pasta appeared in Spain. Pasta making can be traced back to the Arab world, so it could have simply arrived with rice, though it is also likely that Italian cooks travelling to Spain transferred their own love of pasta into Spanish cooking.

Most savoury Spanish dishes begin with a sofrito; a rich paste-like melange of garlic, onion, paprika, saffron and tomato sautéed in oil. Into this other ingredients are stirred and cooked briefly before adding stock, rather than water, to add depth of flavour (see pages 14 and 15 for stock recipes). For traditional paella, a combination of meats, seafood and seasonal vegetables are used, and when cooked, it should be dry on the top, crusty at the bottom and moist in the middle. Fideua, the more current invention, is made with just fish and seafood. It uses less liquid, takes less time to cook and, although it also has a dry top and a crispy base, it is less 'wet' than paella. Both crispy bases are known as socarrat… and are often fought over!

There are many paella and fideua variations to be found in this book, from soups and stews to baked, fried or even sweet dishes. If you plan on making them regularly, I really recommend investing in a 35-cm/14-inch paella pan, even if a shallow flameproof casserole or large frying pan/skillet will do. Baked rice dishes (arroz al horno) are traditionally oven cooked in an earthenware dish (or cazuela), are similar in texture to paella and they, too, are left to sit for 5–10 minutes before serving. You can also cook all the paella recipes in the oven; once all of the ingredients are in the pan, transfer to the oven and cook as specified. Creamy rice (arroz caldozo), similar to risotto, is traditionally cooked in a two-handled pan that is deeper than a paella pan, and is served immediately with alioli, a fiercely Spanish garlic mayonnaise (see page 12). Rice or noodle soups (sopa con arroz y fideos) are cooked in a deep saucepan/pot and require the most liquid. They also need to be served straight away to prevent the rice or noodles absorbing more liquid and becoming mushy. The final two chapters feature some lesser known – compared to paella, that is – but equally impressive recipes for fried dishes (frituras) and sweet dishes (el postre), that can be found in households all over Spain.

If you're a lover of Spanish food, you're sure to find authentic and surprising recipes here.

The Spanish Storecupboard
La Despensa de la Cocina Español

Saffron (azafrán) is the world's most expensive spice. It is the dried stigma of a variety of crocus plant (*Sativus*) and is still picked by hand, which is why it is so expensive. The higher the percentage of pure red rather than red-yellow strands, the better the quality, and both the strands and powdered saffron can be added to a dish. However, if a recipe calls for powdered saffron it is best to use the strands and pound them yourself, to ensure its quality.

Paprika (pimentón) is a powdered spice made from red (bell) peppers that are smoked and dried over a fire, and is one of Spain's finest

and most highly prized commodities. There are many different types of paprika and it is used in everything from chorizo sausage to sauces. Varieties include smoked (ahumado de la Vera), sweet (dulce), hot (picante) and bitter-sweet (agridulce). Of course, the flavour will vary depending on the type, as will the colour, which can range from an orangey rust to a deep burnt red.

Ñora peppers (pimienta ñora) are small, sweet-fleshed red (bell) peppers only available dried. They add flavour to stews and soups and are much more commonly used than chilli/chile peppers, especially in a paella or fideua. To prepare and rehydrate the dried peppers, pierce them with a sharp knife – this allows the

water to penetrate and be absorbed – and soak them in boiling water for about 15 minutes. Discard the stalks and seeds, then scrape the flesh from the skins, reserving the paste and disposing of the skins.

Ñora pepper paste (pasta de pimienta ñora) is now readily available from specialist suppliers, and is far easier and quicker to use than the above method. Both the whole dried pepper and the paste are used in the book, but you can use either in the same quantities.

Espelette peppers (Ezpeletako biperra in Basque) are small red chilli/chile peppers only grown in Espelette and its surrounding villages in Pays Basque, south-west France. With a medium-intense heat, they appear speckled red-orange once ground. They smell a little of hay, yet with a sweet, slightly lemony, smoky flavour, and are used on both sides of the border in French and Spanish Basque dishes. Cayenne pepper can substitute if needs be.

Piquillo peppers (pimientos del piquillo) are small, pointed red chilli/chile peppers grown in Spain, and are only sold roasted and brined in jars or cans. They are commonly used in tapas dishes, stuffed or in salads, but make a delicious addition to rice dishes.

Rice (arroz). Of the two premium varieties grown, Calasparra rice is perhaps the best known outside of Spain, while the even more coveted bomba rice even has Designation of Origin (DO) status as a mark of its unique characteristics. Bomba is a tiny, pearl-shaped grain, with high starch content. It is expensive as rice goes and hard to find outside of Spain, although it can be bought online (see page 128) and in certain stores. If you cannot find bomba or Calasparra rice, arborio risotto rice makes a good substitute.

Noodles (fideos/fideus). In Spain, the generic term for pasta noodles is fideos or fideus, depending on the region, and fideua is the name given to the dish when cooked in a paella pan. Far fewer types of pasta noodles are used in Spain than in Italy, and most recipes call for fideos, a noodle similar to vermicelli but made in short lengths. They are available from specialist food stores or online (see page 128) but you can use vermicelli or angel hair pasta and break it into small lengths, if you prefer. I have found vermicelli already made into short lengths in French and UK supermarkets.

Squid/cuttlefish ink (tinta de calamar/sepia) is the ink that squid and cuttlefish squirt at their predators from sacs in their hind gut. When used in cooking, the flavour is like an intense hit of squid, adding real depth of flavour to dishes. It can be found in specialist fishmongers, but now it is widely available in jars or small sachets as concentrated ink. Arroz a negro or fideua a negro are two of Spain's most famous dishes that use squid ink.

Olive oil (aceite de oliva). Spain is the world's largest producer of olive oil and for many years it was exported to Italy, where it was blended and re-bottled, being sold on as Italian oil. Today, Spanish olive oil is highly regarded in its own right and over 20 varieties have been awarded Designation of Origin (DO). As the recipes in this book use olive oil for frying, I tend to use a good-quality Spanish oil from the supermarket, rather than opting for a very expensive oil that I reserve to drizzle on salads. As Spain produces over half of the world's olive oil, it is quite likely that the oil you have been buying and using at home originated in Spain.

Salt (sal). Spain produces some wonderful artisan sea salt called flor de sal. It is a very flaky, crystalline salt and tastes strongly of the sea; full of nutrients and highly recommended for the dishes in this book.

Chorizo (pronounced chore-reeth-oh) is a type of cured Spanish sausage made from coarsely chopped pork and red (bell) pepper, seasoned with chilli/chili powder and paprika. Available dried and raw, both types add a robust flavour to dishes and are great in paellas, even if some would argue it is not a traditional ingredient. I only use dried chorizo in these recipes, as it is far easier to find.

Mallorcan sausage (sobrasada de Mallorca) is similar to chorizo but is far softer in texture.

Although it is strictly a raw sausage, it is cured and can be eaten without cooking. It is similar to the Italian soft, cured, yet spicy sausage called njuda, which could be used instead. You can substitute it with regular chorizo if you like.

White haricot/navy beans (alubia blanca). The Spanish love legumes both fresh and dried. Used in many different types of regional dishes, this smallish white bean is the most widely grown variety in Spain and is used in many soups and stews. You can substitute with cannellini beans if you need to.

Basic Recipes
Recetas Básicas

As with all cuisines, there are a handful of basic recipes integral to many Spanish dishes. Most savoury dishes begin with a sofrito (see page 7), a vital element of Spanish cooking.

Paella and fideua are often accompanied by alioli, a Spanish garlic mayonnaise. Sometimes stirred through the dish before serving, it adds a creaminess as well as a wonderful hit of garlic umami. Here is a basic alioli recipe with flavour variations, and a vegan version. For both, you can vary the amount of garlic, to your taste. Aside from the ingredients here, other flavours could be used, such as chopped herbs, roasted or puréed (bell) peppers, or even squid ink.

A good home-made stock is also used in all paella and fideua dishes to give a fuller, rounder flavour. They are definitely worth the effort to make as they provide a superior depth of flavour to the dish, and are highly recommended for the recipes in this book (see pages 14 and 15).

Alioli

3 egg yolks

2–4 garlic cloves, crushed

2 teaspoons white wine vinegar

½ teaspoon Dijon mustard

125 ml/½ cup fruity extra virgin olive oil

125 ml/½ cup olive oil

sea salt and ground white pepper

Lemon alioli

grated zest and freshly squeezed juice of ½ lemon

Saffron alioli

a pinch of saffron strands

1 tablespoon boiling water

Harissa alioli

2–3 teaspoons harissa paste

Serves 6

Add more or less garlic depending on what you prefer – either way it will be delicious!

Place the egg yolks, garlic, vinegar, mustard and a little salt and pepper in a bowl and use electric beaters to whisk/beat, until frothy.

In a separate bowl, combine the oils together and gradually add to the yolks a little at a time, beating well after each addition, until the sauce is thickened and glossy and all of the oil is incorporated. It should be able to hold its shape. If the mixture is too thick, thin it with a teaspoon or so of boiling water, until you reach the required consistency.

Variations

Lemon Alioli Follow the basic recipe above, adding the lemon zest to the egg yolks and replacing the vinegar with the lemon juice.

Saffron Alioli Soak the saffron strands in the boiling water for 5 minutes. In the meantime, follow the basic recipe above, then add the saffron strands and the infused water to the alioli and whisk/beat again, until evenly mixed.

Harissa Alioli Follow the basic recipe above, then stir in the harissa paste, to taste.

Vegan Tofu Alioli

250 g/9 oz. silken tofu, drained

2–3 tablespoons tahini paste

2 tablespoons extra virgin
   olive oil

1 garlic clove, crushed

1–2 tablespoons lemon juice

sea salt and freshly ground
   black pepper

Saffron tofu alioli

a small pinch of saffron strands

1 teaspoon boiling water

Serves 4

No need to miss out on this delicious sauce if you are vegan or egg intolerant with this egg-free version of alioli.

Place all the ingredients in a bowl and whisk/beat, until smooth.

Variation

Saffron Tofu Alioli Soak the saffron strands in the boiling water for 5 minutes. In the meantime, follow the basic recipe above, then add the saffron strands and the infused water to the tofu alioli and whisk/beat again, until evenly mixed.

Vegetable Stock

The addition of rice or lentils and mushrooms produces a richly flavoured vegetable stock.

3 tablespoons olive oil

1 onion, chopped

4 garlic cloves, chopped

1 large potato, chopped

1 leek, sliced

2 large carrots, sliced

2 tomatoes, roughly chopped

150 g/5½ oz. mushrooms, chopped

50 g/¼ cup brown rice or green lentils

125 ml/½ cup dry white wine

4 sprigs flat-leaf parsley

2 sprigs thyme

sea salt

a few black peppercorns, lightly bashed

Makes approximately
1.5 litres/generous
6 cups

Heat the oil in a large saucepan/pot and fry the onion and garlic with a little salt for 10 minutes, until lightly golden. Add the potato, leek and carrots and fry for a further 5 minutes.

Add all the remaining ingredients to the pan along with and 2 litres/8 cups of cold water. Bring to the boil and simmer, covered, for 1 hour, skimming the surface to remove any scum.

Strain the stock through a fine-mesh sieve/strainer and season with salt to taste. To enhance the flavour, you can reduce the stock further by simmering it gently. Let cool and use as required, or keep refrigerated for up to 3 days. Alternatively, freeze the cooled stock for up to 3 months.

Chicken Stock

Refrigerating the cooled stock overnight allows the liquid to solidify, leaving a solid layer of fat on top, making it far easier to remove.

2 kg/4½ lb. whole boiling chicken, washed

2 onions, chopped

2 carrots, sliced

2 sticks celery, chopped

2 leeks, sliced

2 garlic cloves

2 teaspoons sea salt

a few sprigs flat-leaf parsley

a few sprigs thyme

a few black peppercorns, lightly bashed

Makes approximately 2 litres/8 cups

Place the chicken in a large saucepan/pot with all of the other ingredients and cover with 2.5 litres/10 cups of cold water. Bring to the boil and simmer gently, partially covered, for 3 hours, skimming the surface to remove any scum. Strain the stock through a fine-mesh sieve/strainer and let cool, then chill overnight.

Carefully skim off the congealed layer of fat from the surface of the stock. Use as required or keep refrigerated and use within 3 days. Alternatively, freeze the cooled stock for up to 3 months.

Fish Stock

When making a fish stock it is important not to boil the ingredients for more than 30 minutes, especially if you are using prawn/shrimp heads, as the resulting stock will become bitter. Ask your fishmonger for some fish trimmings that otherwise get thrown away.

4 tablespoons olive oil

1.5 kg/3 lb. fish trimmings

1 onion, chopped

1 leek, sliced

1 carrot, sliced

1 dried ñora pepper (see page 8), pierced with a sharp knife

a few sprigs flat-leaf parsley

sea salt

a few black peppercorns, lightly bashed

Makes approximately 1.5 litres/generous 6 cups

Heat half of the olive oil in a large saucepan/pot. Add the fish and fry over a high heat, until brown. Remove the fish from pan and set aside. Add the remaining oil to the pan and fry the onion, leek and carrot with a little salt for 5 minutes, until softened.

Return the fish to the pan with 2 litres/8 cups of cold water, the pepper, parsley sprigs and peppercorns. Bring to the boil and simmer, covered, for 30 minutes, skimming the surface to remove any scum.

Strain the stock through a fine-mesh sieve/strainer and let cool. Use as required or keep refrigerated and use within 3 days. Alternatively, freeze the cooled stock for up to 3 months.

Paellas

Paellas

Valencian Paella
Paella Valenciana

Traditionally Valencian paella includes snails, but I have omitted them; for some reason my friends tend not to eat them! If you do wish to add them, you can buy canned snails – you will find them in specialist Spanish or French food shops.

6 tablespoons olive oil

750 g/26 oz. chicken pieces, cut into small portions (see Tip below)

500 g/18 oz. rabbit pieces, cut into small portions (see Tip below)

1 large onion, finely chopped

4 garlic cloves, finely chopped

2 large ripe tomatoes, chopped

2 teaspoons sweet paprika

1/4 teaspoon saffron strands, ground

1.5 litres/generous 6 cups hot chicken stock (see page 15)

500 g/18 oz. mixed beans, such as runner beans, shelled broad/fava beans and cooked butter beans

400 g/generous 2 cups bomba, Calasparra or arborio rice

sea salt

Serves 6–8

Heat half of the oil in a 40-cm/16-inch paella pan (or large shallow flameproof casserole dish). Season the chicken and rabbit pieces with salt and fry, in batches, for 5–6 minutes, until golden on both sides. Remove with a slotted spoon and set aside.

Add the remaining oil to the pan, and fry the onion and garlic for 10 minutes, until softened. Add the tomatoes, paprika and ground saffron, and cook gently for a further 5 minutes, until the mixture is almost dry. Return the meat to the pan and add the hot stock. Simmer gently for 40 minutes, until the meat is tender.

Stir in the mixed beans then add the rice, stirring once, and return to a gentle simmer. Cook for about 20 minutes, until all the stock is absorbed and dry holes start to appear over the surface. Remove the pan from the heat but leave to sit for 10 minutes before serving.

Tip: to cut the chicken and rabbit into small pieces it is best to use poultry shears, or perhaps you could ask your butcher to do this for you.

Chicken and Seafood Paella
Paella con Pollo y Marisco

This is the paella that most people know as Spanish paella, and it can be found in restaurants all over Spain, not always (in fact rarely) as the original Alicante version was intended. This adaptation is as close as I can get in a domestic kitchen. If you cannot find mussels or langoustines, use any other fresh seafood you can buy.

500 g/18 oz. mussels, scrubbed

100 ml/generous ⅓ cup dry white wine

8 raw large prawns/jumbo shrimp, peeled and deveined (see page 97)

8 langoustines (optional)

¼ teaspoon saffron strands

6 tablespoons olive oil

4 skinless chicken thigh fillets, quartered

350 g/¾ lb. prepared squid rings

4 large garlic cloves, crushed

1 red (bell) pepper, seeded and chopped

2 tomatoes, finely chopped

1 teaspoon sweet paprika

350 g/scant 2 cups bomba, Calasparra or arborio rice

200 g/1½ cups fresh or frozen peas

sea salt and freshly ground black pepper

freshly chopped flat-leaf parsley, to garnish

Serves 4

Discard any of the cleaned mussels that do not close when tapped on the work surface. Place the mussels, still wet from cleaning, in a saucepan/pot and place over a medium heat. Add the wine and cook the mussels, covered, for 4–5 minutes, until the shells have opened (discarding any that remain closed). Strain and reserve the liquid to make a stock. Set the mussels aside.

Remove the heads from the prawns/shrimp and langoustines, if using, and add the heads to the mussel liquid along with 1.25 litres/generous 5 cups cold water. Bring to the boil and simmer gently for 30 minutes, skimming the surface to remove any scum. Strain the stock through a fine sieve/strainer into a saucepan/pot (you should have about 1 litre/generous 4 cups), stir in the saffron strands and keep warm.

Heat half of the oil in a 35-cm/14-inch paella pan (or shallow flameproof casserole dish) and fry the chicken pieces for about 5 minutes, until browned. Remove with a slotted spoon and set aside. Repeat with the prawns/shrimp, then the langoustines and finally the squid rings, frying for 2–3 minutes, until golden, removing each with a slotted spoon.

Reduce the heat, add the remaining oil to the pan and gently fry the garlic for 5 minutes, until softened. Stir in the (bell) pepper, tomatoes and paprika, and cook for about 5 minutes, until the sauce is sticky. Stir in the rice and return the chicken to the pan. Add the stock, bring to the boil and simmer gently for 10 minutes.

Stir in the prawns/shrimp, langoustines, mussels, squid and peas, and cook for a further 10 minutes, until the rice and seafood are cooked. Season to taste. Remove the pan from the heat but leave to sit for 10 minutes before serving. Serve sprinkled with chopped parsley.

Seafood Paella with Chorizo
Paella de Marisco y Chorizo

In the north-west of Spain (and Portugal) chorizo sausage is added to many
different dishes, and it is often combined with seafood in paella. This adds
a real depth of flavour to the dish, and you can use either a mild or spicy
sausage, depending on personal preference – I like the spicy variety best.

¼ teaspoon saffron strands

500 g/18 oz. baby clams, scrubbed (see page 94)

250 g/9 oz. mussels, scrubbed

900 ml/3¾ cups hot chicken stock (see page 15)

3–4 tablespoons olive oil

250 g/9 oz. spicy chorizo, thickly sliced

4 strips of pork belly, cut into 3-cm/1¼-inch pieces

250 g/9 oz. raw large prawns/jumbo shrimp, peeled, deveined and heads removed

2 large garlic cloves, crushed

2 ripe tomatoes, finely chopped

350 g/scant 2 cups bomba, Calasparra or arborio rice

sea salt and freshly ground black pepper

Serves 4

Heat the saffron strands in a small dry frying pan/skillet, until lightly toasted.
Set aside. Discard any of the cleaned clams or mussels that do not close
when tapped on the work surface. Transfer them to a large saucepan/pot
and add a splash of water. Cook, covered, over a high heat for 3–4 minutes,
until the shells have opened (discarding any that remain closed). Strain the
shellfish liquid into the stock and stir in the toasted saffron. Set the clams
and mussels to one side.

Heat half of the oil in a 30-cm/12-inch paella pan (or shallow flameproof
casserole dish) and fry the chorizo over a medium heat, until golden and the
fat is released. Remove with a slotted spoon and set aside. Repeat with the
pork belly and fry for 2–3 minutes, then remove and set aside. Sear the
prawns/shrimp for 1 minute on each side, until golden, adding more oil as
necessary. Remove and set aside.

Lower the heat and gently fry the garlic in the pan for 5 minutes. Stir in
the tomatoes and cook over a medium heat for 5 minutes, until the sauce
is quite dry. Return the pork pieces to the pan with the stock, bring to the
boil and then stir in the rice and a little salt and pepper. Simmer gently for
15 minutes. Stir in the prawns/shrimp, clams and mussels, and simmer for
a further 10 minutes, until the rice is al dente and the prawns/shrimp are
cooked. Remove the pan from the heat but leave to sit for 10 minutes
before serving.

Rice with Langoustine
Paella con Langostinos

Classically this luxurious paella would be served with whole langoustines arranged over the rice. I prefer to use the heads and claws to add flavour to the stock, and the halved langoustines are then added to the rice, making them far easier to eat. With strips of piquillo peppers and the pink shellfish, this still looks wonderful as it's brought to the table. You could use large prawns/jumbo shrimp instead.

1.25 litres/generous 5 cups fish stock (see page 15)

20 large langoustines

¼ teaspoon saffron strands

6 piquillo peppers (see page 9)

6 tablespoons olive oil

1 small onion, finely chopped

4 garlic cloves, crushed

grated zest and freshly squeezed juice of ½ lemon

2 tomatoes, finely chopped

1 teaspoon sweet paprika

350 g/scant 2 cups bomba, Calasparra or arborio rice

sea salt and freshly ground black pepper

2 tablespoons freshly chopped flat-leaf parsley, to garnish

Serves 4

Place the stock in a large saucepan/pot. Remove the heads and claws from the langoustines and add to the pan. Bring to the boil and simmer gently for 20 minutes, then strain and discard the shells. Add the saffron strands to the stock and set aside to infuse. Finely chop 1 of the piquillo peppers, and cut the rest into thick strips. Set aside.

Cut the langoustine bodies in half lengthways and discard the black intestinal tract. Heat half of the oil in a 35-cm/14-inch paella pan (or shallow flameproof casserole dish) and fry the langoustines, in batches, for 30 seconds on each side, until lightly golden. Remove with a slotted spoon and set aside.

Add the remaining oil to the pan and gently fry the onion, garlic and lemon zest for 10 minutes, until soft and lightly golden. Add the finely chopped peppers, tomatoes and paprika, and cook for a further 10 minutes, until the sauce is dry.

Add the rice, stir well and then pour in the stock. Cook for 15–18 minutes and then arrange the langoustine halves and thick pepper strips over the rice. Squeeze over the lemon juice, and cook for a further 5 minutes. Remove the pan from the heat but leave to sit for 10 minutes before serving. Serve sprinkled with chopped parsley, and accompanied by some salad leaves, if you like.

Paella with Artichokes and Broad Beans

Paella de Alcachofas y Habas

Driving around the coastal regions of Spain in summer you see fields of artichokes everywhere, so it's hardly surprising to find a rice dish dedicated to this striking vegetable. You really do need to use fresh artichokes here. I have adapted this recipe to include chopped mint and, unusually for paella, to serve it with saffron alioli – it just seems to work.

4 medium artichokes, halved or quartered

1 lemon, halved

4 tablespoons extra virgin olive oil

2 bay leaves, bruised

4 garlic cloves, crushed

1 onion, finely chopped

1.2 litres/5 cups hot vegetable stock (see page 14)

250 g/2 cups shelled and peeled broad/fava beans

350 g/scant 2 cups bomba, Calasparra or arborio rice

2 tablespoons freshly chopped mint

sea salt and freshly ground black pepper

saffron alioli (see page 12), to serve

Serves 4

Start by preparing the artichokes. Cut the stems off to about 2 cm/¾ inch and the leaves down to about 3–4 cm/1¼–1½ inches from the top. Peel away and discard any tough leaves to reveal the round base. In the centre there will be a hairy 'choke'. Scoop this out and discard it. Cut the bases in half and put them into a bowl filled with cold water. Squeeze in the juice from both lemon halves, and put the squeezed halves in the water too.

Heat the oil in a 35-cm/14-inch paella pan (or shallow flameproof casserole dish) and add the bay leaves. Fry gently for about 30 seconds, until fragrant, and then stir in the garlic, onion and a little salt and pepper. Lower the heat and cook for 20 minutes, until the onion is caramelized. Add the artichoke halves and stock, bring to the boil and simmer gently for 10 minutes.

Stir in the broad/fava beans, rice and mint, and simmer gently for 20 minutes, until the rice is al dente and the liquid absorbed. Remove the pan from the heat but let sit for 10 minutes before serving with a bowl of saffron alioli.

Tip: to make individual paella in the oven, follow the above method, until you have added all the ingredients except the alioli. Combine everything and then divide between 4 individual pans. Bake in a preheated oven 200°C (400°F) Gas 6 for about 20 minutes, until the rice is al dente.

Vegetable Paella from Murcia
Paella Hortelana

25 g/scant ¼ cup blanched almonds

4 tablespoons roughly chopped flat-leaf parsley

4 garlic cloves

6 tablespoons extra virgin olive oil

750 g/26 oz. baby vegetables, such as carrots, turnips, fennel, courgettes/zucchini and green beans

1 litre/generous 4 cups hot vegetable stock (see page 14)

150 g/1¼ cup fresh or frozen peas (thawed if frozen)

1 large leek, trimmed and thinly sliced

1 green (bell) pepper, seeded and finely chopped

1 plum tomato, peeled and finely chopped

2 teaspoons sweet paprika

¼ teaspoon saffron strands, ground

350 g/scant 2 cups bomba, Calasparra or arborio rice

sea salt and freshly ground black pepper

courgette/zucchini flowers, sliced, to garnish (optional)

Serves 4–6

Murcia, as well as producing some of the area's best rice, is also the market garden of Spain, which explains why this paella is often known simply as 'paella hortelana' meaning 'paella of the vegetable garden'. Interestingly, this dish often has a pesto-like sauce added to it, made with ground almonds, garlic and flat-leaf parsley. I like to use a selection of baby vegetables, but really any vegetable works well.

To make a parsley pesto, toast the almonds in a dry frying pan/skillet, until dotted brown, then pound them in a pestle and mortar (or a food processor) with the parsley and 2 of the garlic cloves, until finely ground. Stir in 2 tablespoons of the oil. Set aside.

Trim the baby vegetables and halve any larger ones. Bring the stock to the boil and blanch the prepared baby vegetables and the peas for 1–3 minutes, depending on their size. Set the vegetables aside and reserve the stock.

Heat the remaining oil in a 35-cm/14-inch paella pan (or shallow flameproof casserole dish). Crush the remaining garlic and then add it to the pan with the leek, green (bell) pepper and some salt and pepper. Fry gently for 10 minutes, until lightly golden. Add the tomato, paprika and ground saffron, and cook for a further 8–10 minutes, until the sauce is dry and sticky.

Stir the rice and parsley pesto into the pan, until the rice grains are well coated. Pour in the reserved stock, bring to the boil and simmer gently for 15 minutes. Stir in the blanched vegetables and peas and continue to cook for a further 5–8 minutes, until the rice is al dente, the stock absorbed and the vegetables are tender. Season with salt and pepper. Remove the pan from the heat but leave to sit for 10 minutes before serving. Serve garnished with sliced courgette/zucchini flowers, if you like.

Summer Vegetable Paella with Vegan Alioli

Paella de Verduras de Verano con Alioli Vegano

4 tablespoons olive oil, plus extra for brushing

2 garlic cloves, crushed

2 tomatoes, peeled, seeded and finely chopped

1 small fennel bulb, trimmed and very thinly sliced

1 red (bell) pepper, seeded and thinly sliced

1 yellow (bell) pepper, seeded and thinly sliced

2 teaspoons smoked paprika

¼ teaspoon saffron strands

50 ml/scant ¼ cup dry sherry or white wine

300 g/1¾ cups bomba, Calasparra or arborio rice

900 ml /3¾ cups vegetable stock (see page 14)

1 large Little Gem/Bibb lettuce, trimmed and cut into wedges

12 cherry tomatoes

10 chargrilled artichoke hearts, drained (see Tip below)

50 g/½ cup black olives, pitted/stoned, if you like

sea salt and freshly ground black pepper

vegan tofu alioli (see page 13), to serve

Serves 4–6

Served with vegan tofu alioli, this brightly coloured and flavour-packed paella is perfect for summertime. I love the combinations of textures, especially the chargrilled lettuce. You can vary the toppings by choosing from other summer or seasonal ingredients such as courgettes/zucchini and aubergines/eggplants.

Heat the oil in a 35-cm/14-inch paella pan (or a shallow flameproof casserole dish) and fry the garlic for 30 seconds, until it starts to turn golden. Add the tomatoes and a little salt and cook for about 5 minutes, until the tomatoes and oil start to separate.

Add the fennel, (bell) peppers, paprika and saffron, stir well and cook for 10 minutes, until softened. Add the sherry or wine and simmer for 2–3 minutes, until the liquid has cooked off.

Add the rice and stir well, allowing to cook for 2 minutes, then add the stock. Bring to the boil and cook, uncovered, for 20 minutes over a medium–low heat, until the rice is al dente.

Meanwhile, prepare the lettuce. Heat a griddle pan or heavy based frying pan/skillet, until hot. Brush each wedge with a little olive oil and season with salt and pepper. Cook on the heated griddle pan, until each side is charred. Set aside.

Remove the paella pan from the heat and top with the remaining ingredients, including the charred lettuce. Cover with a clean tea/kitchen towel and leave to sit for 5 minutes. Serve with vegan tofu alioli.

Tip: if you can, I recommend finding charred artichoke hearts from a good-quality deli. However, if they are unavailable to you, canned or jarred ones will do.

Country Rabbit and Sobrasada Paella
Paella de Conejo del País y Sobrasada

As soon as you travel inland away from the Spanish coast you begin to see more meat and less fish being used in dishes. Rabbit is hugely popular and a staple of many inland regions; however, chicken can be used instead, if you like – just substitute with an equal amount. Sobrasada is a Mallorcan cured and spiced soft sausage (see page 11) – you can use chorizo instead.

1 litre/generous 4 cups chicken stock (see page 15)

a large pinch of saffron strands

100 ml/generous ⅓ cup olive oil

1 kg/2¼ lb. rabbit or chicken pieces (see Tip, page 18)

250 g/9 oz. brown cap mushrooms, quartered

3 garlic cloves, crushed

1 small onion, finely chopped

75 g/3 oz. Mallorcan sausage (see page 11)

2 tomatoes, peeled, seeded and diced

300 g/1¾ cups bomba, Calasparra or arborio rice

100 g/2 cups baby spinach leaves

sea salt and freshly ground black pepper

lemon wedges, to serve

Serves 4–6

Heat the stock in a small saucepan/pot, until it comes to the boil. Add the saffron, turn off the heat and allow to steep, until required; at least 20 minutes.

Heat one third of the oil in a 35-cm/14-inch paella pan (or shallow flameproof casserole dish). In a bowl, season the rabbit or chicken pieces with salt and pepper. Add to the pan and fry in batches for 5–6 minutes, until evenly browned. Remove from the pan with a slotted spoon and set aside.

Next, add half of the remaining oil to the pan and when hot, stir in the mushrooms. Cook over a high heat for 3–4 minutes, until browned. Remove with a slotted spoon and set aside.

Add the remaining oil to the pan and fry the onion, garlic and a little salt over a medium heat for 10 minutes, until softened but not browned. Add the Mallorcan sausage and cook for 3–4 minutes, stirring and breaking it down, until lightly golden. Stir in the tomatoes and cook for 5–6 minutes, until you have a thick paste.

Pour the saffron-infused stock into the pan and add the rabbit or chicken pieces. Bring to the boil, cover the pan and cook over a low heat for 30 minutes. Remove the rabbit or chicken pieces and set aside.

Stir the rice into the pan until the grains are well coated. Return the rabbit or chicken and the mushrooms to the pan, stirring well. Return the stock to a simmer and cook uncovered over a medium heat for 15–20 minutes, until the rice is al dente. Remove the pan from the heat, scatter the spinach leaves over the rice, cover and leave to sit for 5 minutes, until the spinach is wilted. Stir well and serve with lemon wedges.

Arroz a Banda with Chargrilled Fish
Arroz a Banda con Pescado a la Parrilla

Translating as 'rice on the side', arroz a banda originates from Valencia and its surrounding coastline. Back in the day, fishermen would use up smaller, more bony fish by cooking them in water to make a rich stock, then used to cook their rice. Any edible poached fish would be eaten alongside. Here, rice is cooked in the fish stock from page 15, served with chargrilled dorade.

4 tablespoons olive oil, plus extra for rubbing

4 garlic cloves, crushed

2 tomatoes, peeled, seeded and diced

2 teaspoons smoked paprika

½ teaspoon Espelette pepper (see page 9)

300 g/1¾ cups bomba, Calasparra or arborio rice

¼ teaspoon saffron strands

900 ml/3¾ cups fish stock (see page 15)

4 x 350 g/¾ lb. whole fish such as bream, snapper, dorade or sea bass

sea salt and freshly ground black pepper

lemon wedges, mixed salad leaves and alioli (see page 12), to serve

freshly chopped flat-leaf parsley, to garnish

Dressing

2 tablespoons extra virgin olive oil

1 small garlic clove, finely chopped

1 tablespoon lemon juice

sea salt

Serves 4

Heat the oil in a 35-cm/14-inch paella pan (or shallow flameproof casserole dish). Fry the garlic for 5 minutes, until it just starts to go brown. Add the tomatoes and continue to cook, stirring occasionally for 5 minutes, until the oil and tomatoes start to separate. Stir in the paprika and Espelette pepper and cook for a further 2 minutes.

Next, add the rice and saffron and allow to cook in the paste for 2 minutes, until coated. Add the stock and bring to the boil. Cook for 20 minutes, until the rice is al dente. Remove the pan from the heat and leave to sit for 5 minutes, or until ready to serve.

In a small bowl, combine the dressing ingredients, season with a little salt and set aside.

Meanwhile, heat a griddle pan or heavy based frying pan/skillet, until hot. Score the fish several times each side and rub with a little olive oil, salt and pepper. Cook on the heated griddle pan for 4–5 minutes on each side, until charred and cooked through. Remove from the pan, drizzle with the dressing and leave to sit for 5 minutes.

Serve the paella with the chargrilled fish, lemon wedges, some salad leaves and your favourite alioli. Garnish with a sprinkling of parsley.

Wild Mushroom Paella with Piquillo Peppers

Paella de Champiñones con Pimientos del Piquillo

A rich and hearty rice dish ideally served in autumn/fall when wild mushrooms are at their best and, most likely, locally sourced, although you can make this year round using any mushrooms. The addition of crispy sage leaves isn't traditional, but it is delicious.

15 g/¼ cup mixed dried mushrooms

100 g/3½ oz. piquillo peppers (see page 9)

500 g/18 oz. mixed wild and cultivated mushrooms

60 ml/¼ cup olive oil

4 garlic cloves, crushed

2 teaspoons smoked paprika

2 teaspoons finely chopped sage leaves

grated zest and freshly squeezed juice of 1 lemon

¼ teaspoon saffron strands

2 tomatoes, peeled, seeded and finely chopped

300 g/1¾ cups bomba, Calasparra or arborio rice

900 ml/3¾ cups vegetable stock (see page 14)

sea salt

alioli (see page 12), to serve

Crispy sage leaves

3 tablespoons olive oil

a handful small sage leaves

Serves 4

Place the dried mushrooms in a small bowl and add 100 ml/generous ⅓ cup of boiling water. Set aside to soak for 20 minutes. Drain, reserving the liquid, and finely dice the mushrooms.

Drain and dry the peppers. Finely chop half and thinly slice the remaining peppers, setting the sliced ones aside. Cut or slice the fresh mushrooms so they are all roughly the same size.

Heat half of the oil in a 35-cm/14-inch paella pan (or shallow flameproof casserole dish). Add the fresh mushrooms and stir-fry over a high heat for 3–4 minutes, until evenly golden. Stir in the dried mushrooms and cook for a further 3–4 minutes, until any juices have been cooked off. Remove from the pan and set aside.

Heat the remaining oil in the pan. Add the garlic, chopped piquillo peppers, paprika, sage, lemon zest, saffron and a little salt and fry over a medium heat for 10 minutes, until softened and lightly golden. Add the tomatoes and continue to cook for a further 5 minutes, until you have a paste-like mixture.

Stir in the rice and cook for 1 minute, then add the stock and the reserved mushroom liquid. Bring to the boil and cook over a medium heat for 10 minutes, then stir in the mushrooms and half of the lemon juice. Cook for a further 10 minutes, until the rice is al dente and the liquid absorbed. If you like, add more of the lemon juice to taste.

Remove the pan from the heat, scatter the thinly sliced peppers over the rice, cover the pan and leave to sit for 5 minutes before serving.

For the crispy sage leaves, heat the oil in a small frying pan/skillet and when hot, add the leaves and fry for 1–2 minutes, until golden and crispy. Drain on kitchen paper/paper towels and scatter over the paella. Serve with alioli.

Moorish Paella with Preserved Lemons

Paella de Morisca con Limones en Conserva

Throughout Spain you will find many influences from the Moors, who left behind a love of spices, as well as the introduction of rice in the 8th century. This dish makes the most of both such ingredients in a richly colourful dish; half paella, half pilaf.

60 ml/¼ cup olive oil

50 g/⅓ cup whole raw almonds

1 onion, finely chopped

4 garlic cloves, crushed

2 carrots, thinly sliced

200 g/7 oz. peeled and seeded butternut squash, finely chopped

1 teaspoon ground turmeric

½ teaspoon smoked paprika

¼ teaspoon ground cinnamon

¼ teaspoon saffron strands

½ bunch coriander/cilantro, finely chopped, plus extra leaves to serve

300 g/1¾ cups bomba, Calasparra or arborio rice

900 ml/3¾ cups vegetable stock (see page 14)

50 g/⅓ cup dried cranberries

2 tablespoons sliced preserved lemon peel

sea salt

harissa alioli (see page 12), to serve

Serves 6

Heat half of the oil in a 35-cm/14-inch paella pan (or shallow flameproof casserole dish). Add the almonds and stir-fry over a medium heat for 3–4 minutes, until evenly browned. Remove with a slotted spoon and set aside.

Add the remaining oil to the pan and fry the onion, garlic and a little salt over a medium heat for 5 minutes, until softened. Stir in the carrots, squash, turmeric, paprika, cinnamon and saffron strands and half of the chopped coriander/cilantro. Fry for a further 5–6 minutes, until the carrots and squash are slightly softened.

Add the rice into the pan and cook, stirring constantly, for 2–3 minutes, until the grains are lightly toasted. Add the stock and bring to the boil. Simmer over a medium–low heat for 20 minutes, until the rice is al dente.

Remove the pan from the heat, scatter over the cranberries, preserved lemon, toasted almonds, remaining coriander/cilantro and leave to sit for 5 minutes before serving. Stir together and serve with harissa alioli.

Creamy Rice Dishes
Arroz Caldoso

Rice with Duck and Artichokes
Arroz Caldoso de Pato y Alcachofas

In spring and late summer migrating birds, including ducks, can be found in large numbers at Lake Albufera outside Valencia, in the heart of the rice fields. They make a lovely rich addition to local rice dishes, complemented by artichokes. It is fine to use canned artichokes here.

4 confit duck legs (about 300 g/10½ oz. each)

2 tablespoons olive oil

1 onion, finely chopped

4 garlic cloves, crushed

4 tablespoons canned tomato pulp or chunky passata/ strained tomatoes

1 teaspoon sweet paprika

1.25 litres/generous 5 cups hot chicken stock (see page 15)

400-g/14-oz. can artichoke hearts, drained and halved

350 g/scant 2 cups bomba, Calasparra or arborio rice

4 tablespoons freshly chopped flat-leaf parsley, plus extra to garnish

sea salt

Serves 4

Wipe away and discard the duck fat from the legs, and set aside.

Heat the oil in a flameproof casserole dish and gently fry the onion and garlic for 10 minutes, until softened. Stir in the tomato pulp or passata/ strained tomatoes and paprika and cook for 5 minutes, until dry. Pour in the hot stock.

Stir in the artichoke hearts and rice, and arrange the duck legs in the pan, pressing down into the rice. Return to a gentle simmer and cook for about 20 minutes, until the rice is al dente and the liquid almost absorbed. Stir in the parsley and garnish with an extra sprinkling on top.

Hunter's Rice
Arroz de Caza

It's not hard to imagine the type of ingredients found in this aptly named dish, full of the bounty of a day's hunting, as well as ingredients such as mushrooms and herbs that can be found growing in the countryside. Here these are combined to produce an intense rice dish, ideal for a family gathering. You can use chicken or pork instead of rabbit, if you like.

500 g/18 oz. rabbit pieces, cut into small pieces (see Tip, page 18)

3 quails, cut into quarters

6 tablespoons olive oil

500 g/18 oz. mixed mushrooms, such as oyster, shiitake and brown

2 large garlic cloves, crushed

1 tablespoon each freshly chopped rosemary, sage and thyme, plus extra to garnish

2 tablespoons blanched hazelnuts, toasted and ground

2 tomatoes, finely chopped

2 teaspoons hot paprika

¼ teaspoon saffron strands, ground

1.5 litres/generous 6 cups hot chicken stock (see page 15)

450 g/2¼ cups bomba, Calasparra or arborio rice

sea salt and freshly ground black pepper

crusty bread and a green leaf salad, to serve (optional)

Serves 6–8

Season the rabbit and quail pieces with salt and pepper.

Heat 2 tablespoons of the oil in a flameproof casserole dish and fry the rabbit and quail for 5–6 minutes, until golden brown. Remove with a slotted spoon and set aside.

Add 2 more tablespoons of oil and fry the mushrooms over a high heat for 3–4 minutes, then remove with a slotted spoon.

Add the remaining oil to the pan and gently fry the garlic and herbs for 5 minutes. Add the hazelnuts and cook for 5 minutes. Stir in the tomatoes, paprika and saffron, and fry for a further 5 minutes, until the sauce is dry.

Add the rabbit, quail and mushrooms to the pan, and pour in the hot stock. Bring to the boil and simmer gently for 15 minutes. Stir in the rice and simmer again for a further 15–20 minutes, until the rice is al dente. Sprinkle over some herbs and serve with crusty bread and a crisp green leaf salad, if you like.

Cuban Rice
Arroz Cubano

This Cuban-inspired rice dish, traditionally served at breakfast, is typical of the cross migration of cuisines. The rice is flavoured with bacon and served with a tangy tomato sauce, a fried egg and fried banana! It reminds me of the Indonesian dish, nasi goreng, and it tastes fabulous. Thanks to Ruben, chef during my visit to The Beach at Bude in Cornwall in the south of England, for this recipe.

2 rashers/strips bacon, chopped

250 g/generous 1¼ cups bomba, Calasparra or arborio rice

600 ml/2½ cups hot chicken stock (see page 15)

2 bananas, halved

4 tablespoons seasoned flour

4 eggs

1 tablespoon freshly chopped coriander/cilantro

a few rocket/arugula leaves, to serve

Tomato sauce

4 tablespoons of sunflower oil, plus extra for frying

1 onion, chopped

2 garlic cloves, finely chopped

4 tomatoes, finely chopped

1 teaspoon white wine vinegar

1 teaspoon dried oregano

sea salt and freshly ground black pepper

Serves 4

First, make the tomato sauce. Heat half of the oil in a saucepan/pot and fry the onions and garlic for 20 minutes, until caramelized, adding a little water if necessary to stop the onion burning. Stir in the tomatoes and simmer for a further 20 minutes, until the sauce is thick. Stir in the vinegar and oregano, and season to taste. Set aside and keep warm.

Heat the remaining oil in a frying pan/skillet and fry the bacon for 3–4 minutes, until golden. Stir in the rice and then add the stock. Bring to the boil and simmer gently for 20 minutes, until al dente. Set aside and keep warm.

Dust the bananas with seasoned flour and shallow fry in sunflower oil, in a small frying pan/skillet, for 1–2 minutes on each side, until golden. Remove with a slotted spoon and then fry the eggs until cooked to your liking.

Arrange the rice on serving plates and top each serving with half a banana and a fried egg. Sprinkle with coriander/cilantro and serve immediately with the tomato sauce and some rocket/arugula leaves.

Rice with Lobster
Arroz Caldoso con Langosta

Rice with lobster is typically found in most coastal towns in Spain. The texture of this version reminds me of an Italian risotto; the rice creamy but still slightly al dente. It was inspired by a recent trip to Barcelona, where we enjoyed a Catalan variation, which included ñora peppers and toasted almonds.

6 tablespoons olive oil

1 frozen raw lobster, about 500 g/18 oz., thawed and cut into pieces (see Tip below)

4 garlic cloves

1 small onion, very finely chopped

1 tablespoon roughly chopped flat-leaf parsley

1 tablespoon ñora pepper paste (see page 9)

¼ teaspoon saffron strands, ground

2 tablespoons toasted almonds

1 anchovy fillet, chopped

1 ripe tomato, diced

150 g/generous ¾ cup bomba, Calasparra or arborio rice

500–600 ml/2–2½ cups hot fish stock (see page 15)

sea salt

Serves 2

Heat 4 tablespoons of the oil in a flameproof casserole dish, add the lobster pieces and stir-fry for 2–3 minutes, until golden. Remove with a slotted spoon and set aside.

Add the garlic to the pan and fry gently for 5 minutes, until really softened and golden. Add the onion to the pan, lower the heat and cook gently for 15 minutes, until softened and golden.

Add the parsley, ñora pepper paste, saffron, almonds, anchovy and tomato to the pan, and cook for a further 5 minutes, until the sauce is quite dry. Transfer to a blender and pulse to make a smooth sauce.

Add the remaining oil to the pan, add the sauce and heat through. Stir in the rice and arrange the lobster over the top. Pour in the stock and simmer gently for about 15–20 minutes, until the rice is al dente. Season with salt to taste, and serve at once.

Tip: if you buy frozen raw lobster, thaw it thoroughly in the fridge. Alternatively, buy a live lobster and kill it humanely at home. Freeze the live lobster for 1 hour, until it is almost comatose and still, then place it on a board and firmly insert a sharp knife into the cross on the lobster's head. Quickly split the lobster lengthways in half. To prepare the lobster, place tummy-side up on a board and, using a sharp knife, cut in half straight down through the head and body. Separate the claws and, using claw crackers (or a small hammer), crack the shell lightly. Clean out the soft brown part from the head section and discard. Cut the body into 4 or 5 pieces.

Rice with Squid in Ink
Arroz Negro

Black, unctuous and quite unlike any other rice dish, the flavour of this crazy-looking rice is truly fabulous. You can use either squid or cuttlefish for this recipe, and ask your fishmonger for the small packets of prepared squid ink. You will need 2 small packs or 2 teaspoons. Double the quantities, as required, for more people.

350 g/¾ lb. prepared small squid or cuttlefish (you can use pre-cleaned squid)

4 tablespoons olive oil

2 large garlic cloves, chopped

1 small red (bell) pepper, seeded and diced

1 large tomato, seeded and finely chopped

1 teaspoon smoked paprika

¼ teaspoon saffron strands, ground

1 tablespoon freshly chopped flat-leaf parsley

2 teaspoons squid ink (see page 10)

500 ml/generous 2 cups hot fish or chicken stock (see page 15)

150 g/generous ¾ cup bomba, Calasparra or arborio rice

sea salt and freshly ground black pepper

crusty bread, to serve (optional)

Serves 2

Roughly chop the prepared squid. Heat the oil in a 25-cm/10-inch frying pan/skillet or shallow flameproof casserole dish, and quickly stir-fry the squid for 2–3 minutes, until lightly golden. Remove with a slotted spoon and set aside.

Add the garlic and red (bell) pepper to the pan with a little salt, and fry gently for 10 minutes, until softened. Add the tomato, paprika, saffron and parsley, and cook for a further 5 minutes, until the mixture is quite dry.

Place the squid ink in a bowl and stir in a little of the hot stock. Add the rice to the casserole dish, stir well and then add the squid pieces, inky stock and the rest of the stock. Stir once and then bring to the boil and simmer gently for 20 minutes, until the rice is al dente and the stock is creamy and quite sticky. Season to taste and serve immediately with some crusty bread, if you like.

Rice with Salt Cod
Arroz con Bacalao

Along with their love of rice, the Spanish also have a great fondness for salt cod, and it can be found in dishes all over the mainland and islands in various guises. Naturally enough, there are many recipes that combine these two favourite ingredients. You will need to begin this dish 24 hours before serving.

650–750 g/23–26 oz. salt cod

4 tablespoons olive oil

200 g/7 oz. cooked, peeled prawns/shrimp, finely chopped

4 garlic cloves, chopped

4 tomatoes, seeded and chopped

2 teaspoons ñora pepper paste (see page 9)

1 teaspoon hot paprika

300 g/1¾ cups bomba, Calasparra or arborio rice

1 litre/generous 4 cups hot fish or chicken stock (see page 15)

75 g/½ cup (dark) raisins

2 tablespoons freshly chopped coriander/cilantro

1 tablespoon finely chopped preserved lemon

sea salt and freshly ground black pepper

Serves 4

Place the salt cod in a large bowl of cold water and leave to soak for 24 hours, stirring and changing the water as frequently as you can – perhaps 2–3 times during the day, then last thing at night and first thing the next morning. Once the cod is softened, remove it from the water, rinse it well and carefully discard any skin and bones. Thoroughly dry the pieces of fish on kitchen paper/paper towels. Flake the flesh into bite-sized chunks (you should be left with about 400 g/14 oz.).

Heat half of the oil in a non-stick flameproof casserole dish and fry the fish over a medium heat for 3–4 minutes, until golden. Remove with a slotted spoon and set aside. Repeat with the prawns/shrimp. (If you do not have a non-stick casserole dish, fry the fish in a non-stick frying pan/skillet and transfer to a flameproof casserole dish. Otherwise, the fish will fall apart.) Lower the heat, add remaining oil and gently fry the garlic for 5 minutes, until softened. Add the tomatoes, ñora pepper paste and paprika, and cook over a medium heat for 10 minutes until the sauce is thick.

Stir the rice into the pan, add the stock, bring to the boil and simmer gently for about 15 minutes. Stir in the raisins, salt cod and prawns/shrimp, and cook for a further 5 minutes, until the rice is tender and most of the stock absorbed. Stir in the coriander/cilantro and preserved lemon, and season with salt and pepper. Serve immediately.

Green Rice with Clams
Arroz Verde con Almejas

This dish comes form the Basque region of Spain, where it can be made either with cooked rice, or, as it is here, with cooking the rice as part of the recipe. You could use any fresh clams for this, but small ones work particularly well.

6 tablespoons olive oil

4 garlic cloves, crushed

75 ml/5 tablespoons dry white wine

1 kg/2¼ lb. small clams, scrubbed (see page 94)

1 bunch spring onions/ scallions, trimmed and finely chopped

1 green (bell) pepper, seeded and diced

1 green chilli/chile, seeded and finely chopped

grated zest and freshly squeezed juice of 1 lemon

250 g/generous 1¼ cups bomba, Calasparra or arborio rice

900 ml/3¾ cups hot fish stock (see page 15)

4 tablespoons freshly chopped flat-leaf parsley

sea salt

Serves 4

Heat 2 tablespoons of the oil in a saucepan/pot, add half of the garlic and fry gently for 3–4 minutes, until softened. Add the wine and bring to the boil, then stir in the cleaned clams. Cook, covered, for 4–5 minutes, until all the clams have opened (discarding any that remain closed). Strain and reserve the cooking liquid and set the clams to one side.

Heat the remaining oil in a saucepan/pot and fry the remaining garlic, spring onions/scallions, green (bell) pepper, chilli/chile and lemon zest for 5 minutes, until softened.

Stir the rice into the pan, until the grains are well coated, and then add the clam liquid, stock and half the parsley. Simmer gently, uncovered, for 15 minutes. Stir in the clams and the remaining parsley, and cook for a final 5 minutes, until the rice is al dente. Stir in the lemon juice and serve at once.

Spring Green Paella with Asparagus and Salsa Verde

Paella Verde de Primavera con Espárragos y Salsa Verde

6 tablespoons extra virgin olive oil

1 onion, finely chopped

2 garlic cloves, crushed

2 tomatoes, peeled, seeded and finely chopped

2 teaspoons sweet paprika

¼ teaspoon saffron strands

300 g/1¾ cups bomba, Calasparra or arborio rice

900 ml/3¾ cups vegetable stock (see page 14)

500 g/18 oz. (prepared weight) mixed spring greens, such as shelled peas, shelled broad/fava beans, asparagus spears and fine green beans

sea salt

alioli (see page 12)

a handful of rocket/arugula leaves (optional), to serve

Salsa verde

½ bunch mixed fresh herbs, roughly chopped

1 garlic clove, crushed

1 tablespoon drained capers

4 pitted/stoned green olives, chopped

2 teaspoons lemon juice

½ teaspoon caster/superfine sugar

5 tablespoons extra virgin olive oil

1 tablespoon boiling water

sea salt and freshly ground black pepper

Serves 6

Make the most of the new season's vegetables, using whatever is available, and finish this lovely, creamy paella with a fresh herb salsa. A good balance of flavours would be mint, flat-leaf parsley and coriander/cilantro, but any mix of soft leaves is good.

Heat the oil in a 35-cm/14-inch paella pan (or shallow flameproof casserole dish). Fry the onion, garlic and a little salt over a medium heat for 10 minutes, until lightly golden. Add the tomatoes, paprika and saffron strands and cook for a further 5–6 minutes, until the sauce is dry and sticky.

Stir the rice into the pan, until the grains are well coated, and then pour in the stock. Simmer gently for 15 minutes. Scatter the vegetables over the top of the rice and cook for a further 5 minutes, until the rice is al dente and the vegetables are tender. Remove the pan from the heat, cover and leave to sit for 5 minutes.

Meanwhile, make the salsa verde. Place all the ingredients in a blender and whizz, until as finely chopped as possible.

Stir a little of the alioli through the paella and serve with a spoonful or two of the salsa verde and a handful of rocket/arugula leaves, if you like.

Baked Rice Dishes
Arroz Al Horno

Stuffed Peppers with Chorizo
Pimientos Rellenos de Arroz con Chorizo

I would imagine that this dish was first invented to use up leftover paella, which is often cooked in large quantities. It is, however, delicious in its own right.

1 tablespoon olive oil

50 g/2 oz. mild chorizo, diced

1 small onion, finely chopped

1 large garlic clove, crushed

1 teaspoon freshly chopped thyme

1 large tomato, diced

200 g/generous 1 cup bomba, Calasparra or arborio rice

500 ml/generous 2 cups hot chicken stock (see page 15)

4 red (bell) peppers

sea salt and freshly ground black pepper

Spicy tomato sauce

400-g/14-oz. can chopped tomatoes

2 tablespoons olive oil

1 garlic clove, crushed

a pinch of dried chilli/hot pepper flakes

½ teaspoon caster/superfine sugar

sea salt and freshly ground black pepper

saffron alioli (see page 12), to serve

Serves 4

Preheat the oven to 200°C (400°F) Gas 6.

Start by making the spicy tomato sauce. Place the tomatoes, oil, garlic, chilli/hot pepper flakes, sugar and a little salt and pepper in a saucepan/pot, and bring to the boil. Simmer gently for 15–20 minutes, until thickened. Pour into a 1.5-litre/6-cup baking dish.

Heat the oil in a frying pan/skillet and gently fry the chorizo for 5 minutes, until browned. Add the onion, garlic and thyme to the pan, and fry gently for 10 minutes. Stir in the tomato and a little salt and pepper, and cook for 5 minutes. Then stir in the rice. Add the stock, bring to the boil and simmer gently for about 15–20 minutes, until the rice is al dente with just a little stickiness remaining.

Cut the tops from the red (bell) peppers, reserving the lids. Scoop out the seeds and membrane. Spoon the rice mixture into the (bell) peppers and pop the 'lids' back on. Place in the dish with the sauce, cover with foil and bake in the preheated oven for 1 hour.

Carefully remove the foil and bake for a final 15 minutes, until charred and tender. Remove from the oven and let cool for 30 minutes before serving at room temperature with saffron alioli.

Baked Chicken and Seafood Rice
Arroz al Horno con Marisco y Pollo

A familiar combination in many Spanish rice dishes, any meat, including chicken, and seafood work well together. You can vary the seafood using whatever is available.

1 litre/generous 4 cups hot chicken stock (see page 15)

¼ teaspoon saffron strands

1 tablespoon lemon juice

6 tablespoons olive oil

350 g/¾ lb. skinless chicken thighs, halved (see Tip, page 18)

350 g/¾ lb. raw prawns/shrimp, peeled and deveined (see page 97)

4 garlic cloves

2 bay leaves, crumbled

2 teaspoons sweet paprika

100 ml/generous ⅓ cup canned tomato pulp or passata/strained tomatoes

350 g/scant 2 cups bomba, Calasparra or arborio rice

150 g/1¼ cups frozen peas, thawed

250 g/9 oz. mussels, scrubbed

250 g/9 oz. small clams, scrubbed (see page 94)

sea salt and freshly ground black pepper

3 tablespoons freshly chopped flat-leaf parsley, to garnish

rocket/arugula leaves, to serve (optional)

Serves 6

Preheat the oven to 180° (350°F) Gas 4.

Place the stock, saffron and lemon juice in a saucepan/pot and bring to the boil. Set aside and keep warm.

Meanwhile, heat half of the oil in a 35-cm/14-inch paella pan (or a shallow flameproof casserole dish). Season the chicken pieces with salt and pepper, and fry over a high heat for 4–5 minutes, until golden. Remove with a slotted spoon. Repeat with the prawns/shrimp, stir-frying for 1 minute. Set the chicken and prawns/shrimp aside.

Add the remaining oil to the pan and fry the garlic, bay leaves and paprika for 5 minutes, until fragrant. Stir in the tomato pulp or passata/strained tomatoes and cook for 5 minutes, until dry. Stir in the rice, chicken thighs and warm stock. Bring to the boil and cook over a low heat for 10 minutes.

Stir in the peas, prawns/shrimp and cleaned mussels and clams, pressing well down into the rice. Transfer to the preheated oven and bake for 15 minutes, until the liquid is absorbed. Remove the pan from the oven but leave to sit for 10 minutes before serving, discarding any mussels or clams that have remained closed. Garnish with parsley and serve with some rocket/arugula, if you like.

Baked Rice with Lamb
Arroz al Horno con Cordero

Although it is traditional to use both sausages and meatballs in Spanish rice dishes, this version is one I have adapted to incorporate merguez sausages, because they are just delicious. Better still, rather than making your own meatballs, simply buy some sausages and roll into balls – so quick and easy. You could also use other sausages.

500 g/1 lb. 2 oz. merguez sausages

8 lamb cutlets, French-trimmed (ask your butcher to do this for you)

2 teaspoons dried oregano

3 tablespoons olive oil

1 onion, finely chopped

2 garlic cloves, crushed

250 ml/generous 1 cup passata/strained tomatoes

¼ teaspoon saffron strands, ground

600 ml/2½ cups hot chicken stock (see page 15)

75 g/½ cup (dark) raisins or currants

200 g/generous 1 cup bomba, Calasparra or arborio rice

2 tablespoons freshly chopped mint

sea salt and freshly ground black pepper

Serves 4

Preheat the oven to 200°C (400°F) Gas 6.

Remove the skin from the sausages, divide the sausage meat into 16 pieces and roll into walnut-sized balls. Set aside.

Rub the lamb cutlets with oregano, salt and pepper. Heat half of the oil in a frying pan/skillet and fry the lamb for 5 minutes, until browned all over. Set aside.

Add the remaining oil to the pan and fry the sausage balls for 5 minutes, until browned. Remove with a slotted spoon and set aside.

Add the onion, garlic and a little salt and pepper to the pan, and fry gently for 10 minutes. Add the passata/strained tomatoes, saffron, stock and raisins or currants, and bring to the boil. Stir the rice and mint into the pan and simmer for 5 minutes.

Divide the rice mixture between 4 individual paella pans (or small baking dishes) and top each one with the lamb and sausage balls. Transfer to the preheated oven and bake for about 20 minutes, until the rice is cooked and the stock absorbed. Serve immediately.

Tip: you can make this as one large paella in a 35-cm/14-inch paella pan, and continue as above, baking for a little longer, if required.

Crusted Rice
Arroz con Costra

This is an oven-baked rice dish enriched with a delicious egg crust just before serving. It originates from the Murcia region of Spain, one of the country's most important rice- and vegetable-growing regions. Traditionally this was cooked in a cazuela (see page 7), but a flameproof casserole dish works just as well.

4 tablespoons olive oil

1 head garlic, trimmed but left whole

3 chicken thighs, cut in half (see Tip, page 18)

2 pork belly strips, each cut into 3 pieces (about 250 g/ 9 oz.)

2 tomatoes, diced

1 teaspoon sweet paprika

350 g/scant 2 cups bomba, Calasparra or arborio rice

100 g/3½ oz. black pudding/ blood sausage

400-g/14-oz. can chickpeas, drained

1.25 litres/generous 5 cups hot chicken stock (see page 15)

6 eggs

sea salt and freshly ground black pepper

Serves 6

Preheat the oven to 200°C (400°F) Gas 6.

Heat the oil in a flameproof casserole dish and fry the whole garlic head for 5 minutes, until evenly browned. Add the chicken thighs and pork belly, and fry for 5 minutes, until browned. Remove the meat from the pan with a slotted spoon and set aside (the garlic can stay in).

Add the tomatoes and the paprika to the pan and cook gently for 5 minutes, then stir in the rice so all the grains are coated.

Arrange the chicken, pork and the black pudding/blood sausage in the pan, with the garlic in the middle. Sprinkle over the chickpeas and pour in the stock with a little salt and pepper. Transfer the dish to the preheated oven and bake for 30–35 minutes, until the liquid is absorbed.

Whisk/beat the eggs with a little salt. Remove the pan from the oven, carefully pour over the beaten egg and return to the oven for a further 5 minutes, or until the egg is set, forming a crust. Remove the dish from the oven but leave to sit for 10 minutes before serving.

Baked Rice with Chickpeas and Raisins
Arroz al Horno con Garbanzos y Pasas

It is hardly surprising to find Moorish influences in many of Spain's rice dishes, as it was the Moors who first introduced rice to Spain in the 8th century. Here rice is combined with chickpeas and raisins, as is typical of the sweet/savoury nature of many Moorish recipes. I also like to add a little ground cinnamon to this dish.

5 tablespoons olive oil

1 head garlic, trimmed but left whole

1 small onion, finely chopped

1 large tomato, finely chopped

1 teaspoon sweet paprika

½ teaspoon ground cinnamon

200 g/1½ cups cooked chickpeas, drained

100 g/⅔ cup (dark) raisins

1 litre/generous 4 cups vegetable stock (see page 14)

350 g/scant 2 cups bomba, Calasparra or arborio rice

sea salt and freshly ground black pepper

freshly chopped flat-leaf parsley, to garnish

saffron alioli (see page 12), to serve

Serves 4–6

Preheat the oven to 200°C (400°F) Gas 6.

Heat the oil in a flameproof casserole dish or cazuela (see page 7). Fry the head of garlic over a medium heat for 5 minutes, until golden. Add the onion and lower the heat, fry gently for 10 minutes, then add the tomato, paprika and cinnamon, and cook for a further 5–8 minutes, until the sauce is quite dry. Season with salt and pepper.

Stir in the chickpeas, raisins and stock, and bring to the boil. Add the rice, stir once and return to the boil. Transfer the dish to the preheated oven and bake for about 25 minutes, until the rice is al dente and the stock absorbed. Remove the dish from the oven but leave to sit for 10 minutes before serving with the saffron alioli.

Noodle Dishes
Fideua

Valencian Fideua with Monkfish and Seafood
Fideua Valenciana con Rape y Mariscos

Like paella, fideua originated from the province of Valencia, and its popularity quickly spread to the north of the country, especially Catalonia. Fideua is, however, only served with the addition of seafood, whereas many paella dishes are traditionally a combination of different meats or meat and seafood. This is a typical recipe found in many restaurants around the southern coast of Spain.

5 tablespoons olive oil

350 g/¾ lb. monkfish fillets, cubed

12 raw large prawns/jumbo shrimp, peeled and deveined (see page 97)

1 onion, finely chopped

2 garlic cloves, crushed

2 tomatoes, peeled, seeded and finely chopped

1 red (bell) pepper, seeded and very finely chopped

1 tablespoon ñora pepper paste (see page 9)

2 teaspoons smoked paprika

a pinch of saffron strands

750 ml/3 cups fish stock (see page 15)

300 g/3 cups fideo noodles or vermicelli in short lengths

350 g/¾ lb. mussels, scrubbed

sea salt

alioli (see page 12) and lemon wedges, to serve

Serves 6

Heat 2 tablespoons of the oil in a 35-cm/14-inch paella pan (or shallow flameproof casserole dish) over a high heat. Add the monkfish pieces and fry for 2–3 minutes, until browned. Remove with a slotted spoon and set aside. Add the prawns/shrimp to the pan and fry for 2–3 minutes, until golden. Remove with a slotted spoon and set aside with the monkfish.

Lower the heat to medium. Add the remaining oil to the pan and fry the onion, garlic and a little salt for 10 minutes, until lightly golden. Stir in the tomatoes, red (bell) pepper, ñora pepper paste, paprika and saffron, and cook for a further 5 minutes, until you have a thick paste.

Add the fish stock and noodles, bring to the boil and simmer fast for 6–8 minutes. Press the cleaned mussels into the noodles, then add the monkfish and prawns/shrimp, arranging them over the surface, pressing down gently. Cook for a further 5–6 minutes, until they are heated through and the mussels have opened (discarding any that remain closed).

Remove the pan from the heat but leave to sit for 5 minutes before serving. Serve with some alioli and lemon wedges.

Catalan Squid Ink Fideua
Fideua Catalana con Tinta de Calamar

More than any other ingredient used in both rice and noodle dishes in Catalan cuisine, squid ink (tinta de calamar) is perhaps the most beloved. I, too, love both its intense colour and flavour. I also like to add fennel seeds here for an intriguing, if not traditional, flavour.

1 teaspoon fennel seeds

300 g/10½ oz. small clams such as vongole, scrubbed

500 ml/generous 2 cups fish stock (see page 15)

6 tablespoons olive oil

300 g/3 cups fideo noodles or vermicelli in short lengths

3 garlic cloves, crushed

grated zest and freshly squeezed juice of 1 lemon

2 teaspoons sweet paprika

a pinch of dried chilli/hot pepper flakes

2 tablespoon freshly chopped flat-leaf parsley, plus extra to garnish

2 tablespoons tomato purée/paste

4 sachets squid ink (see page 10), about 1 tablespoon

500 g/18 oz. prepared squid bodies, diced (you can use pre-cleaned squid)

sea salt

saffron alioli (see page 12), to serve

Serves 4–6

Heat a small frying pan/skillet over a medium heat. Add the fennel seeds and toast for 3–4 minutes, until they start to pop and turn brown, releasing their aroma. Cool slightly and then grind to a powder, using either a pestle and mortar or a spice grinder. Set aside.

Place the cleaned clams in a saucepan/pot with a splash of cold water. Cover the pan and cook over a medium heat for 3–4 minutes, until the shells have opened (discarding any that remain closed). Strain and reserve the liquid through a fine sieve/strainer and set the clams aside. Add enough fish stock to the clam liquid to make up to 750 ml/3 cups. Set aside.

Heat half of the oil in a 35-cm/14-inch paella pan (or shallow flameproof casserole dish) over a medium heat. Add the noodles and stir-fry for 3–4 minutes, until golden. Remove from the pan and set aside.

Add the remaining oil to the pan and fry the garlic, lemon zest, paprika, chilli/hot pepper flakes, parsley, ground fennel and a little salt over a low heat for 10 minutes, until softened and lightly golden. Add the tomato purée/paste and squid ink and cook for a further 5 minutes, until the paste is thick, adding a splash of the stock, if the paste is not dissolving.

Stir in the squid and cook for 4–5 minutes, until any juices have evaporated. Add the noodles and stir through the sauce. Add the fish stock and the lemon juice, and bring to the boil and simmer fast for 10–12 minutes, until the noodles are cooked and liquid absorbed.

Remove the pan from the heat and add the clams, pressing them gently into the noodles. Leave to sit for 5 minutes before serving with saffron alioli and garnished with some chopped parsley.

Rossejats de Fideua

Rossejats de Fideua

Loosely translated as 'toasted noodles', fideos were first fried a little in oil before being added to a flavourful stock of poached fish, giving the dish an extra depth of flavour. This all began around the turn of the 20th century when the fisherman would use the 'scraps' of the day's catch to add to the dish, often squid and a few prawns/shrimp. It is a simple, rustic dish, but always served with a bowl of alioli – it is really tasty.

100 ml/generous cup olive oil

300 g/3 cups fideo noodles or vermicelli in short lengths

350 g/¾ lb. prepared squid bodies, chopped (you can use pre-cleaned squid)

12 raw large prawns/jumbo shrimp, peeled, deveined and roughly chopped

2 garlic cloves, finely chopped

1 small onion, finely chopped

2 tablespoons tomato purée/paste

2 teaspoons smoked paprika

a pinch of saffron strands

750 ml/3 cups fish stock (see page 15)

sea salt

freshly chopped flat-leaf parsley, to garnish

lemon wedges and alioli (see page 12), to serve

Serves 6

Heat half of the oil in 35-cm/14-inch paella pan (or shallow flameproof casserole dish) over a medium heat. Add the noodles to the pan and stir-fry for 3–4 minutes, until they turn golden. Remove the noodles from the pan and set aside, wiping the pan clean.

Add the remaining the olive oil to the pan, increase the heat and add the chopped squid, prawns/shrimp and a little salt. Stir well and cook for 2 minutes. Don't scrape the bottom of the pan at this stage as that sticky layer on the bottom is essential for making a rich stock.

Add the garlic and onion and cook for 5 minutes, stirring occasionally, until everything is golden. Add the tomato purée/paste, paprika and saffron, stirring for about 2 minutes, to dissolve the sticky bits on the base of the pan.

Add the stock and bring to the boil. Cook for 5 minutes and then add the noodles. Simmer gently for about 8–10 minutes, until the liquid has been absorbed.

Remove the pan from the heat and leave to sit for 5 minutes to create a toasted layer of noodles in the bottom of the pan. Serve with lemon wedges and a bowl of alioli, and garnish with some chopped parsley.

Canelons
Canelons

4 tablespoons olive oil

1 onion, finely chopped

2 garlic cloves, crushed

2 teaspoons freshly chopped thyme

2 ripe tomatoes, peeled, seeded and finely chopped

250 g/9 oz. pork mince/ ground pork

250 g/9 oz. chicken mince/ ground chicken

50 g/2 oz. chicken livers, finely chopped (optional)

50 g/½ cup dried breadcrumbs

1 egg, beaten

¼ teaspoon grated nutmeg

18 cannelloni pasta tubes

60 g/scant 1 cup grated/ shredded Manchego or Parmesan

sea salt and freshly ground black pepper

tomato salad, to serve (optional)

Bechamel sauce

1 onion, roughly chopped

2 fresh bay leaves

4 whole cloves

900 ml/3¾ cups full/whole fat milk

50 g/2 oz. unsalted butter

50 g/⅓ cup plain/all-purpose flour

sea salt and freshly ground black pepper

Serves 6

Similar to Italian stuffed cannelloni, here the pasta tubes are filled with a mixture of meats and then cooked under a blanket of bechamel sauce. The Italian version normally includes a layer of tomato ragu between the pasta and the white sauce, but this is not so in the Spanish dish. I use grated/shredded Manchego rather than Parmesan, but you can use either, or you can also try Pecorino.

Heat the oil in a medium saucepan/pot over a medium heat and fry the onion, garlic, thyme and a little salt and pepper for 10 minutes, until softened. Stir in the tomatoes and cook for a further 5 minutes.

Increase the heat to high and add the pork, chicken and the livers, if using, and stir-fry for 5 minutes, until golden. Remove the pan from the heat and let cool for 10 minutes. Stir in the breadcrumbs, egg, nutmeg and a little salt and pepper. Set aside to cool completely.

Heat the oven to 200°C (400°F) Gas 6. Lightly oil a 22 x 30 cm/9 x 12 inch (or 2 litre/8 cup) baking dish.

Meanwhile, make the bechamel sauce. Put the onion, bay leaves, cloves, milk and some salt and pepper into a saucepan/pot, bring to the boil and immediately remove from the heat. Set aside to infuse for 20 minutes and then strain using a fine-mesh sieve/strainer.

Melt the butter in a clean saucepan/pot over a medium heat and add the flour and cook, stirring, for 1 minute. Gradually stir in the strained milk and continue to cook, stirring, until the mixture boils and thickens. Simmer for 2 minutes and then remove from the heat. Set aside to cool or use as required (if setting aside, always cover the surface of the sauce with clingfilm/plastic wrap to prevent a skin forming).

Spoon the mince/ground meat filling into the cannelloni tubes and arrange side-by-side, in a single layer, in the prepared dish. Pour the bechamel sauce over the tubes, making sure they are all covered with sauce, and scatter over the cheese. Transfer the dish to the preheated oven and bake for 40 minutes, until the mixture is bubbling and golden, and the pasta al dente. Serve with a tomato salad, if you like.

Catalan Vegetable Stew with Crispy Fideua

Menestra de Verduras con Fideua Crujiente Catalana

125 g/¾ cup dried haricot/navy beans, soaked in water overnight

90 ml/generous ¾ cup olive oil

1 onion, finely chopped

1 large carrot, diced

2 garlic cloves, crushed

1 red (bell) pepper, seeded and diced

2 tablespoons tomato purée/paste

1 teaspoon sweet paprika

1½ teaspoons ground cumin

1 medium potato, peeled and cubed

1 litre/generous 4 cups vegetable stock (see page 14)

150 g/1¼ cups green peas, fresh shelled or frozen

100 g/2 cups shredded spinach leaves

50 g/½ cup fideo noodles or vermicelli in short lengths

½ teaspoon Espelette pepper (see page 9)

sea salt

alioli (see page 12), to serve (optional)

Serves 4

Meat stews are commonplace in Spain, especially in rural areas, but it is rare to find just vegetable stews. I wanted to create something that combined hearty winter veg with fideo noodles, so here is a recipe with both. The noodles are fried and tossed with spices and salt before being scattered over the finished dish. They add a lovely crisp texture.

Drain the soaked haricot/navy beans, discarding the water. Rinse well and place in a large saucepan/pot. Add enough water to cover well and then bring to the boil. Simmer fast for 10 minutes, then reduce the heat and simmer gently for 40–50 minutes, until the beans are tender but not mushy. Drain the beans and then rinse again, discarding the liquid. Set aside.

Heat 2 tablespoons of the oil in a clean saucepan/pot and fry the onion, carrots, garlic, (bell) pepper and a little salt for 10 minutes, until softened. Add the tomato purée/paste, paprika and cumin and cook for a further 5 minutes, until fragrant. Stir in the beans and potato.

Add the stock and bring the soup to the boil. Simmer, covered, for 30 minutes, until the vegetables are cooked. Add the peas and spinach leaves and simmer for a further 5 minutes.

Meanwhile, heat the remaining oil in a small frying pan/skillet to a medium heat and add the noodles. Stir for 2–3 minutes, until crisp and golden. Remove the noodles with a slotted spoon and drain on kitchen paper/paper towels. Transfer to a small bowl and stir in the Espelette pepper and a little salt.

Divide the soup between bowls and top each one with the crispy noodles. Serve with a bowl of alioli, if you like.

Mexican Noodles with Chilli, Lime and Coriander

Fideos Mexicanos con Chile, Lima y Cilantro

We can clearly see examples of Spanish cuisine in all the Spanish-speaking countries, including in Mexico and their dishes, like this variation of a fideua. Ancho chilli/chili peppers are to Mexicans what ñora peppers are to Spanish cooks. Both are only available dried and have a slightly sweet, smoky flavour. They can be bought from specialist suppliers (see page 128).

1 dried ancho chilli/chile pepper

50 ml/scant ¼ cup olive oil

1 onion, finely chopped

4 garlic cloves, crushed

grated zest and freshly squeezed juice of 2 limes

4 sprigs coriander/cilantro, finely chopped, plus extra to garnish

2 red (bell) peppers, seeded and sliced thinly

½ teaspoon ground cumin

a good pinch of saffron strands

300 g/3 cups fideo noodles or vermicelli in short lengths

750 ml/3 cups vegetable stock (see page 14)

sea salt

harissa alioli (see page 12), chilli/chili jam/jelly (see page 108) and lime wedges, to serve

Serves 6

Soak the ancho chilli/chile pepper in plenty of boiling water for 15 minutes. Remove the chilli/chile from the water, discard the seeds and stalk, and carefully scrape the soft flesh from the inside of the skin, discarding the skin. Set the chilli/chile flesh paste aside.

Heat the oil in a 35-cm/14-inch paella pan (or shallow flameproof casserole dish) over a medium heat and fry the onion, garlic, lime zest and chopped fresh coriander/cilantro for 10 minutes, until softened. Add the (bell) pepper, cumin, saffron, chilli/chile paste and a little salt and cook, stirring, for a further 10 minutes.

Add the noodles to the pan and stir well for 1 minute. Add the stock and lime juice, and bring to the boil and simmer over a medium–low heat for 10–12 minutes, until the liquid is absorbed and the noodles al dente.

Remove the pan from the heat but leave to sit for 5 minutes before serving. Serve scattered with coriander/cilantro, a bowl of harissa alioli, some chilli/chili jam/jelly and some lime wedges.

Soups
Sopas

Rice Soup with Chicken and Peppers
Arroz con Pollo y Pimientos

This is a soupy rice dish made with sweet red Romano peppers. If you can find these elongated sweet peppers with pointed tips, use them, or you can use the more common (bell) pepper.

6 tablespoons olive oil

500 g/18 oz. chicken thighs, halved (see Tip, page 18)

1 onion, finely chopped

1 large (or 2 small) red Romano pepper(s) or (bell) pepper(s), seeded and sliced

2 ripe tomatoes, diced

100 ml/generous ⅓ cup dry white wine

1.5 litres/generous 6 cups hot chicken stock (see page 15)

¼ teaspoon saffron strands, ground

4 tablespoons roughly chopped flat-leaf parsley

3 garlic cloves

250 g/generous 1¼ cups bomba, Calasparra or arborio rice

sea salt and freshly ground black pepper

Serves 4–6

Heat 2 tablespoons of the oil in a saucepan/pot over a medium–high heat, season the chicken with salt and pepper, and add to the oil. Brown on all sides for 5 minutes, then remove with a slotted spoon and set aside.

Add 2 tablespoons more to the pan and fry the onion and pepper(s) for 5 minutes. Add the tomatoes and wine, and simmer for a further 5 minutes. Return the chicken to the pan, and add the stock and ground saffron. Bring to the boil, then simmer gently for 15 minutes.

Pound the parsley and garlic together using a pestle and mortar, and stir in the remaining oil to make a paste. Stir half of the parsley-garlic paste into the pan along with the rice. Simmer gently, uncovered, for about 15 minutes, until the rice is al dente. Season to taste, then divide the soup between bowls and serve immediately with the extra parsley-garlic paste.

Mallorcan 'Dirty' Rice
Arroz Brut

1 teaspoon each sea salt and
  freshly ground black pepper

½ teaspoon ground cinnamon

½ teaspoon ground cloves

a little freshly grated nutmeg

¼ teaspoon saffron strands,
  ground

6 tablespoons olive oil

2 chicken thighs, halved
  (see Tip, page 18)

2 pork belly strips, roughly
  chopped, about 250 g/9 oz.

1 small onion, finely chopped

3 garlic cloves, crushed

2 ripe tomatoes, diced

1.25 litres/generous 5 cups
  hot chicken stock (see
  page 15)

125 g/4½ oz. chicken livers,
  chopped (optional)

1 tablespoon freshly chopped
  flat-leaf parsley

100 g/3½ oz. button
  mushrooms, halved

100 g/¾ cup fine green beans,
  chopped

100 g/2⅔ cups frozen peas,
  thawed

150 g/generous ¾ cup bomba,
  Calasparra or arborio rice

Serves 4

It is the combination of different spices that gives this Mallorcan soup its rather worrying name, but don't be discouraged; it tastes wonderful. It is, of course, the spices that also give the soup its flavour, quite unusual in Spanish dishes but pointing to its Moorish origin.

Start by combining the salt, pepper, cinnamon, cloves, nutmeg and saffron in a small bowl, and set aside.

Heat half of the oil in a saucepan/pot and, when hot, fry the chicken and pork for 5 minutes, until evenly browned. Remove with a slotted spoon and set aside.

Add the remaining oil to the pan and gently fry the onion, 2 of the garlic cloves and the prepared spice mixture for 10 minutes. Return the chicken and pork to the pan. Stir in the tomatoes and stock, bring to the boil and simmer gently for 30 minutes.

Combine the remaining crushed garlic clove with the chicken livers (if using) and parsley. Stir into the soup with the mushrooms, beans, peas and rice. Cook for a further 15 minutes, until the rice is al dente. Divide the soup between bowls and serve immediately.

Valencian Rice with Turnips and Beans

Arroz con Nabos y Judías Blancas

If you drive through the rice fields surrounding Lake Albufera on the outskirts of Valencia, you will come across lots of small restaurants all vying for custom. This soup is typical of the area and the recipe here was given to us by our host, José – thank you.

500 g/18 oz. uncooked, smoked gammon knuckle/ ham hock

2 bay leaves

100 g/generous ½ cup dried haricot/navy beans, soaked in cold water for 12 hours

4 tablespoons olive oil

250 g/9 oz. small turnips/ rutabaga, quartered or diced

250 g/9 oz. carrots, diced

4 garlic cloves, left whole

2 teaspoons ñora pepper paste (see page 9)

2 teaspoons smoked paprika

¼ teaspoon saffron strands

150 g/generous ¾ cup bomba, Calasparra or arborio rice

250 ml/generous 1 cup passata/strained tomatoes

4 small black pudding/blood sausages, about 200 g/7 oz.

sea salt

freshly chopped flat-leaf parsley, to garnish

Serves 4–6

Put 2 litres/8 cups cold water into a large saucepan/pot with the gammon knuckle/ham hock and bay leaves. Bring to the boil and simmer for about 30 minutes, skimming the surface to remove any scum.

Drain the soaked haricot/navy beans, discarding the water. Rinse well and add them to the pan. Bring to the boil and simmer for a further 45 minutes, until the beans are cooked. Remove the gammon, finely shred the meat and discard the bone.

Heat the oil in a clean saucepan/pot over a medium heat and gently fry the turnips/rutabaga, carrots, garlic and a little salt for 10 minutes. Stir in the ñora pepper paste and the paprika and saffron, and cook for 1 minute. Stir in the rice.

Add the beans and their cooking liquid, passata/strained tomatoes, black pudding/blood sausage and the shredded meat, bring to the boil and simmer gently for 15 minutes, until the rice is al dente. Divide the soup between bowls and serve garnished with chopped parsley.

Spinach, Rice and Bean Soup
Sopa con Arroz, Espinacas y Judias Blancas

I like to serve this wintery soup with chargrilled sourdough rubbed with garlic and a halved tomato – a traditional Spanish side dish known as pan con tomate. You can allow dinner guests to rub their toasted bread with the garlic and tomato halves themselves, if you like.

2 tablespoons extra virgin olive oil, plus extra to serve

125 g/4½ oz. pancetta or smoked bacon, diced

1 onion, finely chopped

2 garlic cloves, crushed

1 tablespoon freshly chopped rosemary

grated zest and freshly squeezed juice of ½ lemon

150 g/generous ¾ cup bomba, Calasparra or arborio rice

400-g/14-oz. can haricot/navy beans, drained

1.5 litres/generous 6 cups hot chicken stock (see page 15)

350 g/7 cups spinach

sea salt and freshly ground black pepper

Tomato bread

6 slices sourdough bread

2 tablespoons extra virgin olive oil

1 garlic clove

3 tomatoes, halved

sea salt and freshly ground black pepper

Serves 6

Heat the oil in a large saucepan/pot over a medium heat and fry the pancetta or bacon for 5 minutes, until golden. Add the onion, garlic, rosemary and lemon zest to the pan with a little salt and pepper, and fry gently for 5 minutes, until the onion is softened. Stir in the rice and beans, and add the stock. Bring to the boil and simmer gently for 15 minutes.

Meanwhile, wash and dry the spinach leaves, discarding any thick stalks. Shred the leaves. Stir the spinach into the soup with the lemon juice and cook for a further 5 minutes, until the rice is al dente and the spinach wilted.

Next, make the tomato bread. Brush the sourdough slices with a little oil and cook on a ridged griddle pan, until toasted on both sides. Remove the sourdough slices from the pan and rub all over with the garlic clove and then the cut side of the tomatoes. Season to taste.

Season the soup to taste and then divide between bowls. Drizzle over a little olive oil and serve immediately with the tomato bread.

Clam Soup
Arroz Caldoso con Almejas

Many years ago I was eating at a small restaurant near the port in Palma, Mallorca, where I sampled a simple, but nonetheless delicious clam stew. It is the inspiration for this soup, in which I have used rice instead of beans. To clean clams, scrub them under running water or soak them in cold water with a little bran or wheat germ for an hour or so before cooking.

1 kg/2¼ lb. small clams, scrubbed (see above)

1.25 litres/generous 5 cups fish or vegetable stock (see pages 14 and 15)

3 tablespoons extra virgin olive oil

150 g/5½ oz. pancetta or smoked bacon, diced

1 small onion, chopped

2 garlic cloves, chopped

1 tablespoon freshly chopped rosemary

400-g/14-oz. can chopped tomatoes

2 teaspoons hot paprika

150 g/generous ¾ cup bomba, Calasparra or arborio rice

1 bay leaf

sea salt

2 tablespoons freshly chopped flat-leaf parsley, to garnish

crusty bread, to serve

Serves 4

Place the cleaned clams in a small saucepan/pot with just the water that remains on the shells. Cover and cook the clams over a medium heat for 4–5 minutes, until all the shells have opened (discarding any that remain closed). Strain the clam cooking liquid into the stock and warm the stock through. Set the clams aside.

Meanwhile, heat the oil in a saucepan/pot over a medium heat and fry the pancetta for 5 minutes, until browned. Add the onion, garlic, rosemary and a little salt to the pan and fry for 5 minutes, until lightly golden. Add the tomatoes and paprika, and fry gently for a further 10 minutes, until the sauce is quite dry.

Stir the rice into the pan to coat the grains and add the stock and bay leaf. Bring to the boil and simmer gently for 15 minutes. Stir in the clams and heat through for 5 minutes. Divide the soup between bowls, sprinkle with chopped parsley and serve with some crusty bread.

Seafood Rice Soup
Arroz Caldoso de Marisco

I simply can't get enough of piquillo peppers. These little pointed chilli/chile peppers are grown in pots in northern Spain, near the town of Lodosa. They are just 7.5 cm/3 inches in length, and are roasted over embers, giving them a sweet, smoky flavour. They are often stuffed and served as tapas, but I love the piquant flavour they add to this dish. They can be found in jars from large supermarkets or specialist food stores or delis.

4 large langoustines

350 g/¾ lb. raw prawns/shrimp, peeled

1.5 litres/generous 6 cups hot fish stock (see page 15)

6 tablespoons olive oil

100 g/3½ oz. spicy chorizo, chopped

250 g/9 oz. prepared squid rings

1 small onion, finely chopped

4 garlic cloves, crushed

2 tomatoes, finely chopped

50 g/2 oz. piquillo peppers (see page 9), finely chopped

1 teaspoon sweet paprika

¼ teaspoon saffron strands, ground

150 g/generous ¾ cup bomba, Calasparra or arborio rice

sea salt

crusty bread, to serve

Serves 4

First, prepare the seafood. Cut the heads from the langoustines and prawns/shrimp and reserve. Cut the langoustine bodies in half and discard the black intestinal vein. Cut down the back of each prawn/shrimp and discard the black intestinal vein.

Bring the stock to the boil, add the langoustine and prawn/shrimp heads, and simmer gently for 30 minutes, skimming the surface to remove any scum. Strain the stock through a fine-mesh sieve/strainer into a clean pan and keep hot.

Heat half of the oil in a saucepan/pot and fry the chorizo for 3–4 minutes, until crisp and golden. Remove with a slotted spoon and set aside. Add the langoustines to the pan and stir-fry for 1 minute, until golden. Remove with a slotted spoon and set aside. Repeat with the prawns/shrimp, and then the squid.

Add the remaining oil to the pan and fry the onion, garlic and a little salt for 10 minutes, until softened and golden. Stir in the tomatoes, piquillo peppers, paprika and saffron. Cook for 5–6 minutes, until the sauce is quite dry.

Add the rice, stir well and pour in the hot stock. Return to the boil and simmer gently for 10–15 minutes. Add the langoustines, prawns/shrimp and squid and cook for a further 5 minutes, until the rice is al dente and the shellfish are cooked. Divide the soup between bowls and sprinkle over the crispy chorizo. Serve immediately with some crusty bread.

Broth, Pasta and Meatball Soup
Sopa de Galets

Meatballs

150 g/5½ oz. pork mince/
  ground pork

150 g/5½ oz. beef mince/
  ground beef

1 garlic clove, crushed

2 tablespoons dried
  breadcrumbs

1 tablespoon freshly chopped
  flat-leaf parsley, plus extra
  to serve

1 teaspoon freshly chopped
  thyme

200 g/2 cups medium pasta
  shells

sea salt and freshly ground
  black pepper

Manchego or Parmesan,
  grated/shredded, to serve

Broth

1 cooked chicken carcass
  or small chicken (see Tip
  below)

2 chunky short beef ribs

any ham hock or other beef or
  chicken bones you have
  (optional)

1 onion, chopped

1 leek, chopped

1 turnip/rutabaga, swede or
  potato, chopped

2 bay leaves

2 sprigs flat-leaf parsley

1 teaspoon sea salt

Serves 6

The success of this soup lies in the quality of the stock, so this one is made with chicken, beef and pork for maximum flavour. The pasta shells and meatballs can either be cooked separately in the broth or, like here, the shells are stuffed with the raw meat mixture before being cooked. I used a medium-sized shell, about 2 cm/⅔ inch across, but you can substitute with larger ones, if you wish.

Start by making the broth. Place all the ingredients in a large saucepan/pot with 3 litres/12 cups water (or enough to cover everything). Bring to the boil and simmer gently over a low heat for 4 hours, skimming the surface to remove any scum. Strain through a fine sieve/strainer and let cool slightly.

Return the broth to the saucepan/pot, bring back to boil and reduce, until you have about 2 litres/8 cups remaining. Set aside.

For the meatballs, place the pork, beef, garlic, breadcrumbs, parsley, thyme and salt and pepper in a bowl, and mix together thoroughly with your hands. Take the pasta shells one at a time and press in enough of the meatball mixture to fill. Roll any remaining mixture into small meatballs, roughly the same size as the filled shells.

When ready to serve, bring the reserved broth to the boil. Add the stuffed shells (and any meatballs) and cook for 15–20 minutes, until the pasta is al dente and the meat is cooked. Divide the soup between bowls and serve immediately with grated/shredded Manchego or Parmesan.

Tip: you can use the cooked carcass from a roast chicken, or otherwise you could cook the whole bird in the stock.

Spanish Chicken Noodle Broth
Caldo Español de Fideos con Pollo

One of the world's most travelled soups, chicken and noodle broth can be found in cuisines globally, and Spain is no different. There is something so wholesome about eating home-made chicken broth, you almost feel more vibrant afterwards and to be honest, just a little bit smug!

1 small chicken, about
  1 kg/2¼ lb.

2 onions, chopped

2 carrots, chopped

2 leeks, sliced

4 garlic cloves, chopped

2 bay leaves

2 tablespoons olive oil

2 medium potatoes, peeled
  and cubed

100 g/1 cup fideo noodles or
  vermicelli in short lengths

sea salt and freshly ground
  black pepper

1 tablespoon freshly chopped
  flat-leaf parsley, to garnish

Serves 4–6

Place the chicken in a large saucepan/pot and add 1 chopped onion, 1 chopped carrot, 1 sliced leek, half the chopped garlic and the bay leaves. Add 2 litres/8 cups of cold water and bring to the boil. Simmer gently, covered, for 1 hour, skimming the surface to remove any scum.

Strain the stock through a fine sieve/strainer into a bowl, discarding the vegetables, but reserving the chicken. Allow to cool for 30 minutes, until the chicken is cool enough to handle. Then shred the chicken, discarding the skin. You will need about 500 g/18 oz. meat for this recipe. Set the chicken aside.

Meanwhile, heat the oil in a clean saucepan/pot over a medium heat and fry the remaining onion, carrot, leek and garlic, with a little salt and pepper for 10 minutes, until softened. Add the potatoes and stock, and bring to a simmer. Cover and cook for 15 minutes.

Add the shredded chicken to the pan along with the noodles. Cook, uncovered, for a further 5 minutes, until the noodles and vegetables are cooked. Divide the broth between bowls and serve scattered with chopped parsley and a sprinkling of black pepper, if you like.

Tip: keep any leftover chicken and use as a sandwich filling or with green salad leaves.

Fried Dishes

Frituras

Fried Paella with Alioli
Arroz Frito con Alioli

2 tablespoons olive oil, plus extra for brushing

1 small onion, finely chopped

4 garlic cloves, crushed

100 g/3½ oz. smoked bacon, finely diced

2 tomatoes, finely chopped

1 teaspoon sweet paprika

250 g/generous 1¼ cup bomba, Calasparra or arborio rice

600 ml/2½ cups hot chicken stock (see page 15)

1 egg, beaten

sea salt and freshly ground black pepper

sliced avocado, tomato and mesclun salad, and alioli (see page 12), to serve

Spicy chilli/chili oil

2 tablespoons extra virgin olive oil

a few drops of Tabasco sauce

Serves 4

This is another great way to use up leftover paella (or, alternatively, prepare the rice as follows) by adding beaten egg, shaping the rice mixture into 'cakes' and frying on a flat griddle. I like to serve this for brunch with a drizzle of spicy oil, avocado, alioli and salad leaves.

Heat the oil in a large frying pan/skillet and fry the onion, garlic, bacon and a little salt and pepper for 10 minutes, until the onion is softened. Stir in the tomatoes and paprika, and cook for a further 5–10 minutes, until the mixture is dry. Stir in the rice to coat the grains and then add the stock. Simmer gently for about 20 minutes, until the rice is al dente. Remove from the heat and let cool.

Preheat the oven to 150°C (300°F) Gas 2.

When the rice mixture is cold, beat in the egg. Using wet hands, form the mixture into 8 flat cakes. Brush the cakes with oil and cook, in batches, on a hot flat griddle or heavy frying pan/skillet for 5 minutes on each side, until browned and heated through. Keep warm in the preheated oven.

To make the spicy chilli/chili oil, combine the extra virgin olive oil with a little Tabasco.

Arrange the paella cakes on serving plates, spoon on a little alioli, top with sliced avocado and a tomato and mesclun salad. Serve drizzled with the chilli/chili oil.

Paella Arancini with Romesco Sauce
Arancini de Paella con Salsa Romesco

2 tablespoons olive oil

4 garlic cloves, crushed

I tomato, finely chopped

I teaspoon sweet paprika

200 g/7 oz. cooked, peeled prawns/shrimp, finely chopped

200 g/generous I cup bomba, Calasparra or arborio rice

600 ml/2½ cups hot chicken stock (see page 15)

3 eggs

4–6 tablespoons plain/all-purpose flour

100 g/1¼ cups dried breadcrumbs

sea salt and freshly ground black pepper

Romesco sauce

I tablespoon each blanched almonds and blanched hazelnuts, roughly chopped

5 tablespoons extra virgin olive oil

2 large garlic cloves, chopped

I ripe tomato, diced

I small slice of bread, about 25 g/I oz., crusts removed

I roasted red (bell) pepper from a jar, about 100 g/3½ oz.

I tablespoon red wine vinegar

¼ teaspoon Espelette pepper (see page 9)

sunflower oil, for deep frying

Makes 16

Similar to Italian arancini, these deep-fried paella balls are lovely as an appetizer or tapas served with the wonderfully piquant romesco sauce. This version uses paella with prawns/shrimp, but any type of paella (without any bones or shells) could be used in the same way.

Heat the oil in a 25-cm/10-inch paella pan (or shallow flameproof casserole dish) and fry the garlic over a low heat for 5 minutes, until softened. Add the tomato, paprika and a little salt and pepper, and cook for 5 minutes. Stir in the prawns/shrimp, then the rice. Add the stock, bring to the boil and simmer gently for 20 minutes, until the rice is al dente and the stock absorbed. Let cool, then chill the paella for I hour.

Meanwhile, make the sauce. Gently fry the almonds and hazelnuts in 2 tablespoons of the oil, until golden, then remove with a slotted spoon. Add the garlic to the pan and fry for 5 minutes, until softened, then add the tomato and cook for a further 5 minutes. Transfer the tomato mixture to a blender or food processor, add the nuts, bread and red (bell) pepper, and blend, until smooth. Gradually whisk/beat in the remaining oil and the vinegar to make a smooth sauce. Add the Espelette pepper and some salt to taste.

Beat I of the eggs and work into the chilled rice mixture, until combined. Shape into 16 balls about the size of golf balls. Beat the 2 remaining eggs and place in a shallow dish. Dust each ball lightly with flour, dip into the egg and then coat with breadcrumbs.

Put some sunflower oil in a wok or deep saucepan/pot to about 5 cm/2 inches in depth. Heat it, until a cube of bread added to the oil crisps in 20 seconds, then add the balls a few at a time, and fry for 4–5 minutes, turning halfway through, until golden brown. Drain on kitchen paper/paper towels and repeat with the remaining balls. Serve with the romesco sauce.

Fideua Croquettes with Alioli and Chilli Jam

Croquetas de Fideua con Alioli y Mermelada de Chile

I often have leftovers from a pasta or rice supper, so having a recipe with which to make the most of them is ideal. These croquettes are very similar to arancini but use noodles rather than rice. The recipe for basic fideua can be found on page 112 if you haven't got any left over from the day before.

500 g/18 oz. cooked fideua (see page 112)

1 large egg, beaten

50 g/2 oz. Manchego, finely grated/shredded

100 g/1¼ cups dried breadcrumbs

saffron alioli (see page 12) and a rocket/argula or green leaf salad, to serve

Chilli/chili jam/jelly, Spanish style

250 g/9 oz. ripe tomatoes, roughly chopped

2 garlic cloves, chopped

100 g/½ cup caster/superfine sugar

35 ml/2½ tablespoons sherry or red wine vinegar

2 teaspoons ñora pepper paste (see page 9)

1 teaspoon smoked paprika

a pinch of cayenne pepper

½ teaspoon sea salt

Serves 6–8

Start by making the chilli/chili jam/jelly. Place the tomatoes and garlic in a food processor and process, until fairly smooth. Transfer to a saucepan/pot, and add the remaining ingredients, bring to the boil and simmer gently for 10–15 minutes, stirring occasionally to prevent the sauce sticking, until thick and jam/jelly-like. Set aside to cool.

Next, make the croquettes. Place the cooked fideua in a bowl and stir in the egg and cheese. Taking a large spoonful at a time and using lightly damp hands, shape the mixture into 5-cm/2-inch croquettes or short rolls.

Place the breadcrumbs in a shallow bowl and dip in the croquettes, one at a time, rolling to coat completely in the crumbs. Chill for 20 minutes.

Preheat the oven to 150°C (300°F) Gas 2.

Heat a deep saucepan/pot with about 5 cm/2 inches of vegetable oil, until it reaches 170°C/350°F on a sugar thermometer (or until a cube of bread added to the oil crisps in 20 seconds). Cook the croquettes in batches for 3–4 minutes, turning them over several times with a slotted spoon or tongs, making sure they do not become too dark.

Remove from the pan and drain on kitchen paper/paper towels. Keep warm in the preheated oven, until all of the croquettes are cooked. Serve with saffron alioli, the chilli/chili jam/jelly and a simple rocket/argula or other green leaf salad.

Fideua Tortilla
Tortilla de Fideua

This recipe is based on a classic Italian dish, frittata di maccheroni, adapted here to make a Spanish version of tortilla. It can be served as a light lunch or supper dish with alioli and salad, or cut into bite-size pieces and served with romesco sauce (see page 107), as tapas.

200 g/2 cups fideo noodles or vermicelli in short lengths

50 ml/scant ¼ cup olive oil

1 onion, finely chopped

2 garlic cloves, crushed

½ teaspoon smoked paprika

2 eggs, beaten

50 g/2 oz. Manchego, finely grated/shredded, plus extra to serve

2 tablespoons freshly chopped flat-leaf parsley

sea salt

alioli (see page 12), to serve

Serves 8

Bring a medium saucepan/pot of lightly salted water to the boil, add the noodles and cook for 3–4 minutes, until al dente. Drain well, refresh under cold water and drain again. Place in a large bowl and set aside.

Meanwhile, heat half of the oil in a 22-cm/9-inch frying pan/skillet over a medium heat. Fry the onion, garlic, paprika and a little salt for 10 minutes, until soft and golden, then add to the bowl of noodles with the eggs, cheese and parsley. Stir well until everything is evenly mixed.

Add the remaining oil to the pan/skillet and, when hot, pour in the noodle and egg mixture. Cook over a high heat for 10 minutes, then gently flip over and cook for a further 6–8 minutes, until set. Cut the tortilla in the pan/skillet or gently tip it out onto a wooden board and let cool before cutting. Serve with alioli and a sprinkling of Manchego.

Breakfast Fideua Hash Pancakes with Poached Eggs
Panqueques de Desayuno de Fideua Hash con Huevos Escalfados

Another great use of any leftover fideua is to cook it in pancakes. In case you don't have any leftovers, here is a very simple base recipe to follow. This can also be used in the recipe for fideua croquettes on page 108.

Fideua

5 tablespoons olive oil

200 g/2 cups fideo noodles or vermicelli in short lengths

2 garlic cloves, finely chopped

½ small onion, finely chopped

2 tablespoons tomato purée/paste

2 teaspoons smoked paprika, plus extra to serve

a pinch of saffron strands

500 ml/generous 2 cups chicken or vegetable stock (see pages 14 and 15)

lemon alioli (see page 12), avocado wedges and salad leaves, to serve

Pancakes and eggs

cold fideua (see above)

1 tablespoon malt vinegar

4 eggs

Serves 4

First, make the fideua. Heat 2 tablespoons of the oil in a medium frying pan/skillet over a medium heat. Add the noodles and stir-fry for 3–4 minutes, until golden. Remove from the pan and set aside.

Add a further 2 tablespoons of the olive oil to the pan/skillet and fry the garlic and onion for 5 minutes, stirring occasionally, until golden. Add the tomato purée/paste, paprika and saffron and cook for a further 5 minutes, until the mixture forms a paste.

Add the reserved noodles and stock to the pan/skillet and bring to the boil. Simmer over a medium–high heat for 10–12 minutes, until the noodles are cooked and liquid absorbed. Remove from the heat and set aside, until cold.

Preheat the oven to 150°C (300°F) Gas 2.

Next, make the pancakes. Heat the remaining oil in a non-stick frying pan/skillet over a high heat. Divide the cold fideua mixture into 4 equal parts. One part at a time, drop the mixture into the pan to form a flat pancake about 15 cm/5½ inches across, pressing down well with a fish slice. Cook over a medium–high heat for 3–4 minutes, flipping over so that each side of the pancake is crispy and browned. Transfer to a warm plate and keep warm in the preheated oven while cooking the remaining pancakes.

Bring a small saucepan/pot of water to a rolling boil and add the vinegar. Gently crack 2 eggs into the water and poach, until cooked to your liking. Remove with a slotted spoon and keep warm in a covered bowl while cooking the remaining 2 eggs.

Remove the pancakes from the oven and top each one with some alioli, a poached egg, avocado wedges and some salad leaves. Serve immediately with a little smoked paprika scattered over.

Sweet Dishes
El Postre

Baked Saffron Rice Pudding
Arroz con Leche y Azafrán al Horno

There is something truly comforting about eating baked rice pudding. Perhaps it's the fond memories of childhood desserts, or the soft, creamy texture of the dish. This version offers an intriguing hint of saffron. If you want, you can add some dried raisins or currants before baking and serve topped with a drizzle of cream and whatever fresh fruits are in season.

125 g/¾ cup bomba, Calasparra or arborio rice

1 litre/generous 4 cups full-fat/whole milk

75 g/6 tablespoons caster/superfine sugar

1 vanilla pod/bean, split

a pinch of saffron strands

25 g/1⅔ tablespoons butter, diced

single/light cream and seasonal fruits, to serve (optional)

Serves 4

Preheat the oven to 150°C (300°F) Gas 2 and grease a 1.5-litre/6-cup baking dish.

Wash the rice in a sieve/strainer, shake well and place in the prepared dish. Place the milk, sugar, vanilla pod/bean and saffron strands in a saucepan/pot and bring to the boil. Remove from the heat and leave to infuse for 5 minutes.

Scrape out the inner seeds of the vanilla pod/bean and stir them into the milk (discarding the vanilla pod/bean), then pour the milk over the rice. Bake the dish in the preheated oven for 30 minutes.

Remove the dish from the oven and stir well, carefully dot the top with butter and bake for a further 1 hour, until the top of the pudding is golden brown. Lift a little of the skin with the point of a knife; the sauce should be thick and creamy. Cook for longer if required.

Remove the dish from the oven but leave to sit for 10 minutes before serving with some cream and fresh fruits, if you like.

Rice Pudding with Caramel Oranges
Arroz con Leche y Naranjas Caramelizadas

Rice pudding can be found in homes and restaurants all over Spain, especially in Asturias and northern areas, where dairy products are produced. Every region varies the ingredients slightly, and in the north, the dish is often flavoured with lemon and cinnamon, and enriched with egg yolks or butter. I have added my own twist with sliced oranges in syrup flavoured with Pedro Ximénez, a delicious Spanish sweet sherry. Best served at room temperature.

1.5 litres/generous 6 cups full-fat/whole milk

grated zest of 1 lemon

1 cinnamon stick, lightly bashed

150 g/generous ¾ cup bomba, Calasparra or arborio rice

75 g/6 tablespoons caster/superfine sugar

2 egg yolks

Caramel oranges

4 small Valencian oranges

75 g/6 tablespoons soft light brown sugar

4 tablespoons water

2 tablespoons Pedro Ximénez (or other sweet sherry)

Serves 6

Place the milk, lemon zest and cinnamon in a saucepan/pot and slowly bring to the boil. Stir in the rice and sugar, and simmer fast for 5 minutes. Lower the heat and cook very gently, stirring occasionally, for about 45 minutes, until the rice is really soft and creamy. Discard the cinnamon stick.

Remove the pan from the heat and let cool for 10 minutes, then beat in the egg yolks. Spoon the creamy rice into 6 glasses or dishes, let cool then chill in the fridge, until required. (You will need to return them to room temperature for 1 hour before serving.)

Meanwhile, prepare the oranges. Pare the zest of 1 of the oranges into thin strips and squeeze its juice into a small saucepan/pot. Stir in the brown sugar and water and heat gently, stirring, until the sugar is dissolved. Stir in the shredded orange zest and simmer for about 5 minutes, until the sauce is syrupy. Remove the pan from the heat and stir in the sherry.

Peel the remaining 3 oranges and cut them into slices. Arrange the slices in serving bowls. Pour the hot syrup over the orange slices and leave, until cold.

To serve, remove the rice from the fridge and bring to room temperature for 1 hour, then serve topped with the caramel oranges.

Chocolate Rice Pudding with Candied Orange

Pudin de Arroz con Leche de Chocolate y Naranja Confitada

This dish reminds me of a baked chocolate custard; creamy and rich.
The addition of the Grand Marnier and orange zest isn't traditional,
but it transforms this dessert into a real gem.

80 g/½ cup bomba, Calasparra
 or arborio rice

750 ml/3 cups full-fat/whole
 milk

250 ml/generous 1 cup water

50 g/lightly packed ¼ cup soft/
 packed brown sugar

2 tablespoons good-quality
 organic cocoa powder, plus
 extra to dust (optional)

1 tablespoon Grand Marnier
 (or other orange liqueur)

½ teaspoon vanilla essence/
 pure vanilla extract

vanilla ice cream, to serve

Candied orange

1 orange

60 ml/¼ cup water

60g/¼ cup caster/superfine
 sugar

Serves 6–8

Start by making the candied orange. Peel the orange zest and using a small knife cut it into thin julienne strips. Add the caster/superfine sugar and water to a small saucepan/pot and heat gently, stirring, until the sugar is dissolved. Bring to the boil, add the orange zest and simmer for about 15 minutes, until the zest is really softened and almost translucent. Set aside in a bowl and let cool completely.

Meanwhile, rinse the rice and place it in a medium saucepan/pot with the milk and water. Heat gently, stirring, until it comes to the boil. Reduce the heat and simmer gently for 20 minutes, stirring every 5 minutes.

Next, add all the remaining ingredients to the pan and continue to stir for a further 10 minutes, until the rice is al dente and you reach the desired consistency. It should be like a thick pouring custard.

Spoon the rice pudding into dishes and set aside to cool. Serve at room temperature topped with vanilla ice cream and the reserved candied orange. Dust with a little cocoa powder, if you like.

Saffron and Cardamom Noodle Pudding with Pistachio Nuts and Poached Fruits

Pudin de Fideos con Leche de Azafrán y Cardamomo con Pistachos y Frutas Escalfados

I first came across this recipe at Moro, a restaurant in London specializing in dishes from southern Spain and north Africa. Similar to a rice pudding but with noodles, it is – excuse the pun – extremely moreish. You can serve it with any poached fruits.

25 g/1⅔ tablespoons butter

100 g/1 cup fideo noodles or vermicelli in short lengths

650 ml/scant 3 cups full-fat/whole milk

200 ml/generous ¾ cup double/heavy cream

75 g/6 tablespoons caster/superfine sugar

a pinch of saffron strands

½ teaspoon ground cardamom

grilled/broiled or poached fruits (such as peaches or pears) and 2 tablespoons chopped pistachio nuts, to serve

Serves 6

Melt the butter in a deep frying pan/skillet or saucepan/pot over a medium heat. Add the noodles and cook, stirring, for 5 minutes, until golden brown. Stir in the milk, cream, sugar, saffron strands and cardamom and heat gently, until it comes to the boil. Reduce the heat and simmer gently, stirring, until the noodles are cooked; about 5–6 minutes.

Spoon the mixture into 6 glasses or dishes, let cool then chill in the fridge, until required. Serve topped with some grilled/broiled or poached fruits and the pistachio nuts.

Tip: if you can't find ground cardamom, just use 3 green cardamom pods. Remove the seeds from the pods (discarding the pods) and crush them as finely as you can using a pestle and mortar or a spice grinder.

Crispy Baked Noodle Pudding with Honey and Lemon
Pudin de Fideos Crujientes al Horno con Miel y Limón

If you are a fan of a British bread and butter pudding, then you will be in for a treat here. What is basically a sweet 'mac 'n' cheese' is transformed into something much more with raisins and honey. The cooled baked pudding is then cut into fingers, coated in cinnamon crumbs and fried, until crisp and golden. Serve it bathed in freshly squeezed lemon juice, honey and cream – it's divine.

250 g/9 oz. macaroni noodles

25 g/1²⁄₃ tablespoons butter, melted

250 g/9 oz. cream cheese

125 ml/½ cup double/heavy or thick cream

100 ml/generous ⅓ cup honey, plus extra to serve

grated zest of 1 lemon

60 g/⅓ cup raisins

oil, for frying

lemon wedges and double/heavy or single/light cream, to serve

Coating

50 g/¼ cup dried breadcrumbs

2 tablespoons brown sugar

a pinch of ground cinnamon

Serves 8

Preheat the oven to 180°C (275°F) Gas 4 and grease a 22-cm/9-inch square baking dish. Cook the noodles as per the packet instructions. Drain well and set aside.

Combine the butter, cream cheese, cream, honey and lemon zest in a bowl and whisk/beat together, until smooth. Stir in the cooked noodles and the raisins, until evenly combined.

Spoon the mixture into the prepared dish and bake for 30–35 minutes, until firm to the touch and golden. Let cool and then chill overnight in the fridge.

The next day, remove the pudding from the fridge 1 hour before frying.

Combine the coating ingredients on a plate.

Carefully upturn the pudding onto a chopping board, removing it from the baking dish, and cut into 16 fingers. Dip the pieces into the coating, lightly encasing them all over.

Heat a shallow layer of oil in a large, non-stick frying pan/skillet and fry the fingers for 5–6 minutes, turning frequently, until golden on all sides, and warmed through.

Arrange on plates with lemon wedges and serve with a drizzle of honey and cream.

Index

Suppliers and Stockists

UK

Sous Chef
www.souschef.co.uk
Ingredients, equipment, tableware
and gifts inspired by leading
restaurants and international
food, including Spanish goods.

Brindisa
www.brindisa.com
Offers an exceptional selection
of Spanish foods including bomba
rice, fideo noodles, Mallorcan
sausage and other meats, and
many more essential ingredients
mentioned in this book.

Delicioso
www.delicioso.co.uk
Sells squid/cuttlefish ink, ñora
pepper paste and other high-
quality Spanish storecupboard
and deli goods.

Fratelli Camisa
www.camisa.co.uk
This online delicatessen may be
predominantly Italian but it's great
for Spanish cured meats and a
good selection of olive oils and
other basic ingredients.

Seasoned Pioneers
www.seasonedpioneers.co.uk
Stocks a wide range of spices
and seasonings, including smoked
paprika and organic Spanish saffron.

Divertimenti
www.divertimenti.co.uk
Professional quality cookware and
tableware, including paella pans.

Waitrose
www.waitrose.com
High street store that stocks a
selection of Manchego, piquillo
peppers and more, including
Bomba rice.

US

Amigo Foods
www.amigofoods.com
A wide choice of Latin foods,
including Spanish meats, rice,
seasonings and oils.

Delicias de España
www.deliciasdeespana.com
Stocks a good range of Spanish
foods and dishes.

The Spanish Table
www.spanishtable.com
For cazuela cooking pots, Serrano
ham, Manchego and more.

La Tienda
www.tienda.com
Sells sweet smoked paprika,
piquillo peppers, chorizo cooking
sausage, among other Spanish
treats.

Le Creuset
www.lecreuset.com
A favourite brand specializing
in premium cookware including
paella pans and kits, and much
more.

Sur La Table
www.surlatable.com
Great assortment of quality
kitchen goods and basic
storecupboard ingredients
including oils, rice, paella pans,
and even paella workshops at
their stores across the US.